THE THREE HUMANITIES

The Division of Humanity in Yahuah's Plan

Volume 1

Dr. Yeral E. Ogando

COPYRIGHT PAGE — THE THREE HUMANITIES™

© [2025-2026] Dr. Yeral E. Ogando.

All rights reserved.

No part of this publication may be reproduced, stored in a retrieval system, or transmitted in any form or by any means—electronic, mechanical, photocopying, recording, or otherwise—without prior written permission from the publisher, except for brief quotations in reviews or academic works, which must include proper citation.

This book is part of the multi-volume series THE THREE HUMANITIES, including:

Volume 1: The Division of Humanity in Yahuah's Plan

- Book One: The 22 Works of Creation
- Book Two: The First Humanity
- Book Three: The Second Humanity

Volume 2: The Restoration of the First Humanity in Yahuah's Plan

- Book Four: The Third Humanity
- Book Five: The Restoration

All characters, events, narrative structures, diagrams, terminology systems, and original frameworks—including but not limited to The Three Equations of Humanity, The Six Layers of Sheol, The Variant Concept, The Purity Lineage Model, The 22 Works Chart, and the full Three Humanities Narrative Map—are the intellectual property of the author and may not be reproduced, adapted, or distributed without written authorization.

All Scripture quotations appear in their respective translations as noted from Dabar Yahuah Scriptures (www.yahuahbible.com) and are used within fair-use guidelines. Any restored names, spellings, and linguistic transliterations are the author's scholarly preference and form part of the proprietary theological framework of this series.

Published by:

Christian Translation LLC

www.yahuahdabar.com

[USA]

ISBN (Paperback): 978-1-946249-37-1

Cover design, interior layout, charts, and diagrams by Dr. Yeral E. Ogando and affiliated creative teams.

Printed in USA

TABLE OF CONTENTS

Dedication	6
Book 1:	5
Introduction	7
Chapter 1 : Understanding the Divine Foundation of All Things	9
Chapter 2: The Great Work of the Firmament	21
Chapter 3: The Four Great Works of Creation	27
Chapter 4: The Three Great Works of the Fourth Day	33
Chapter 5: The Three Great Works of the Fifth Day	44
Chapter 6: The Creation of the Earthly Realms: Beasts, Cattle, Creeping Things, and the Primordial Behemoth	52
Chapter 7: The Creation of Man and Woman: Spirit Before Body, Body Before Union, Union in the Second Week	57
Chapter 8: Sanctification of the Shabbâth	62
Chapter 9: The Perfect Work of Yahuah Êlôhîym — His 22 Works, His 7 Days, His Eternal Seal	72
Book 2:	77
Introduction	78
Chapter 1: The First Humanity: Qadosh From The Beginning	81
Chapter 2: The Two Kinds Of Humanity	85
Chapter 3: The Origin Of Disobedience	90
Chapter 4: The Half-Truth Of The Nachash	94
Chapter 5: "Like One Of Us": Knowledge, Not Corruption	98
Chapter 6: The Expulsion From Eden: The First Act Of Mercy	102
Chapter 7: The Separation Of Light And Darkness Among Men	105
Chapter 8: The Patriarchal Line Of The First Humanity	109
Chapter 9: The Purity Of The First Humanity Before The Flood	121
Chapter 10: The Prophetic Purpose Of The First Humanity	125

Chapter 11: The Hidden Preparation For The Coming Conflict	129
Book 3:	**135**
Introduction	137
Chapter 1: The Nature Of The Second Humanity	139
Chapter 2: The Inheritance Of The Second Humanity	144
Chapter 3: Why The Second Humanity Has No Redemption	148
Chapter 4: The Mercy Of Yahuah Amid Rising Corruption	151
Chapter 5: The Two-Part Redemptive Plan Of Yahuah	154
Chapter 6: After The Flood: The Giants Rise Again	160
Chapter 7: Scripture Follows The Pure Line, Not The Hybrid One	167
Chapter 8: The Error Of Qeynan (Kenan)	171
Chapter 9: The Nephilim After The Flood	175
Chapter 10: The Three Equations Of Humanity	179

BOOK 1
THE THREE HUMANITIES

The 22 Works of Creation and the Foundation of Yahuah's Redemptive Plan

Dedication

To Ôlâm Êlôhîym — Yahuah Tsâbâ

This work is dedicated first and forever to Yahuah, the Creator of all humanity — the One who shaped Adam from the dust, breathed life into his nostrils,

and whose mercy has preserved us from Eden to this very day.

To Yahusha ha'Mashiyach, the Restorer of all things, whose blood shattered the chains forged by the Nephilim and whose resurrection guarantees the redemption of every nation.

And to every seeker of truth —

to those who refuse to accept tradition over Scripture,

to those who hunger to understand the ancient paths,

and to those who long to see the plan of Yahuah with clarity and reverence.

This book is for you.

May these pages strengthen your faith, sharpen your discernment, and draw you closer to the heart of the Father.

Introduction

The Three Humanities — The Nephilim Corruption and the Eternal Restoration in Yahusha

Humanity has walked through three ages, three identities, and three spiritual conditions since the beginning of creation. Each era reveals a profound truth about Yahuah's justice, mercy, and redemptive plan. Yet for generations, these truths have been obscured by tradition, theology, and the loss of the ancient worldview preserved in the Scriptures and the writings of the patriarchs.

This book opens the first of three volumes, peeling back the veil on a story older than Eden and more relevant than ever before. Here we revisit the first humanity, the world before corruption — a humanity created in purity, righteousness, and perfect fellowship with Yahuah. We explore what truly happened in the Garden, the nature of free will, the meaning of disobedience, and the spiritual structure of creation that governed the earliest generations.

Contrary to modern teachings, humanity was not shaped by inherent wickedness nor born into unavoidable depravity. Instead, the Scriptures reveal a different narrative:

the fall introduced disobedience, not corruption — and corruption only entered later through the rebellion of the Watchers and the birth of the Nephilim.

This volume restores what tradition has forgotten.

It invites the reader to see the ancient world as Yahuah described it, not as later interpretations framed it.

It reveals the original purpose of mankind, the structure of the heavenly order, and the first steps of the divine plan that would ultimately lead to Yahusha ha'Mashiyach — the One who restores what was lost.

As you journey through these pages, prepare to challenge assumptions, rediscover ancient truths, and witness the extraordinary mercy of Yahuah unfolding across the ages. This is more than a historical exploration — it is a return to the foundation of faith, identity, and creation itself

Chapter 1

Understanding the Divine Foundation of All Things

1.1 – WHY WE BEGIN WITH THE 22 WORKS OF CREATION

Before we can understand the First Humanity—its glory, its mandate, its fall—we must return to the very beginning, to the moment when Yahuah spoke reality into existence. The Scriptures reveal that the world was not formed by accident, chaos, or celestial violence. It was shaped by Speech—by the living Words that came from Êlôhîym Himself.

According to the ancient Hebrew understanding and the witness of the Book of Jubilees, creation unfolded through twenty-two distinct divine utterances. Each word was intentional. Each word established a boundary, an order, a law, a function. Each word carried the power of life. These 22 Words of Creation form the spiritual DNA of the universe, the foundation of the first humanity, the structure of all divine law, and the original harmony the Nephilim later sought to corrupt.

If we want to understand what humanity lost—and what Yahusha came to restore—we must first understand what Yahuah built. That is why Book One begins not with Adam, but with the Words that shaped Adam's world. Before we meet the first man... before we see the Garden... before we witness the first disobedience... we step into the beginning. Where Êlôhîym said, and it was so. Now, let us enter the First Day.

1.2 DAY 1 — THE SEVEN GREAT WORKS OF CREATION

(Jubilees 2:2–3 and Bereshith 1 — Dabar Yahuah Scriptures)

Jubilees 2:3 tells us:

"...for seven great works He did create on the first day."

Jubilees 2:2 then lists everything created, and from this list we extract the seven works of creation performed on Day 1.

1.3 – WORK 1: CREATION OF THE SHAMAYIM (THE HEAVENS) – AND THE PRIMORDIAL EARTH

Jubilees 2:2 — "He created the shamayim which are above..."

Bereshith 1:1 — "In the beginning Êlôhîym created the shamayim..."

This is not simply the sky; it is the entire heavenly order: the highest heaven (the Throne of Yahuah), the middle heavens (angelic realms), and the lower heavens (the visible sky). In Hebrew thought, shamayim is plural — meaning layers, realms, dimensions of heavenly existence.

Before the physical world became visible, Yahuah established His throne, His Kingdom structure, His heavenly court, the dwelling places of the righteous, and the realms where His malakim operate.

Yahuah establishes the heavenly Kingdom before the physical world, proving that His sovereignty precedes creation, His government is eternal, and earth is meant to be a reflection of heaven. Yahusha later teaches: "Your will be done on earth as it is in heaven." Because heaven existed first, and earth was created to mirror it.

1.4 EARTH CREATED WITH THE HEAVENS (NOT A SEPARATE WORK)

Jubilees 2:2 — "...and the earth..."

Bereshith 1:1–2 — "He created... the earth. And the earth was without form and void..."

Earth is NOT a separate work of creation. It is created at the exact same moment as the heavens. The "earth" at this stage is not dry land; it is the unformed foundation, the primordial mass submerged under all waters before Yahuah divides the waters.

This unformed earth is created but not shaped, present but not revealed, matter without form, and the raw foundation on which all later works build. Yahuah always creates the substance before forming the structure: matter before shape, earth before Eden, humanity before covenant, Adam before Chawwâh, Noah before the ark, Abraham before the covenant, Yasharal before Torah, and Yahusha before the resurrection. This reveals His nature: Creation → Formation → Fulfillment.

1.5 – WORK 2: CREATION OF THE WATERS

Jubilees 2:2 — "...and the waters..."

These waters include the upper waters (above the heavens), the lower waters (covering the earth), and the deep abyss (tehom).

Bereshith 1:2 — "And the rûach of ĚLÔHÎYM moved upon the face of the waters.."

The very first elements of creation testify that life will flow only from Yahuah.

1.6 – WORK 3: CREATION OF ALL THE ANGELS AND SPIRITS THAT SERVE BEFORE HIM

A revelation Bereshith does not detail.

Jubilees 2:2 — "...and all the spirits which serve before Him..."

A. Angels of the Presence

The highest-ranking malakim — those who stand before Yahuah's throne. Examples in Scripture: Gabrîyêl, Mîykâêl, Râphâêl, Ûrîyêl, Kerûb, Śârâph, Ôphân, Galgal, îyr (the watchers before the fall), and the seven spirits before His throne (Revelation).

B. Angels of Sanctification

They minister holiness, purification, and sacredness. They prepare places, people, and moments for Yahuah's presence.

C. Angels of the Elements (12 categories)

Jubilees lists angels appointed over fire, wind, clouds, darkness, snow, hail, frost, voices, thunder, lightning, cold, heat, and the four seasons.

D. Spirits of All Creatures

"...and of all the spirits of His creatures which are in the shamayim and on the earth..."

This means every living thing already had its assigned spirit, its function, its purpose, its order, and its heavenly counterpart. Bereshith focuses on the physical; Jubilees exposes the spiritual infrastructure. Day 1 is not merely matter being created — it is the creation of spiritual administration itself.

1.7 – WORK 4: CREATION OF THE SPIRIT OF MAN

This is part of the same revelation in Jubilees 2:2 but deserves distinction because of its theological weight: Every spirit of every single man and woman from creation to the end was created on the first day. This means our spirits existed before our bodies, our spirits existed before time shaped our generation, and many spirits waited thousands of years before becoming living souls. It is a great wonder to know that our spirits were created on the first day, inside the heavenly blueprint of Yahuah.

1.8 – WORK 5: CREATION OF THE ABYSSES AND THE FOUNDATIONS OF SHEOL

Yôbêl (Jubilees) 2:2 — "He created the abysses and the darkness..."

On the first day, Yahuah not only created the Light, but also the deep structure that would sustain His plan of redemption: the abysses (tehôm), the darkness (ḥoshekh), and the foundations of Sheol in the inner earth.

Bereshith (Genesis) 1:2 confirms this:

"And the earth was without form, and void; and darkness was upon the face of the deep (tehôm)."

1.9 – THE ABYSS (TEHÔM) AS THE FOUNDATION OF THE UNDERWORLD

The tehôm is the deep, the structural foundation beneath the visible creation. Already in creation week, Yahuah established not only the visible world, but the invisible foundations where judgment, justice, and waiting souls would be placed.

Enoch testifies:

1 Enoch 17:6 — "I saw the deep abyss, with columns of heavenly fire..."

1 Enoch 18:11–13 — "This place is the prison of the angels... until the completion of their judgment."

The abysses created on the first day become the geographical and spiritual base for Sheol and its chambers.

1.10 – THE INNER EARTH DIVISIONS (SHEOL) PREPARED FROM THE BEGINNING

It may sound surprising, but as the perfect Architect, Yahuah also established the full structure of Sheol from the beginning. There are many misconceptions about "hell." In Scripture, Sheol = the inner-earth realm of the dead. It has multiple chambers and functions. It is ordered, not chaotic. It is part of Yahuah's perfect plan of justice and salvation. All these layers are within the earth, one beneath the other. Chănôk (Enoch) Chapter 22.

The Six Main Layers (from top to bottom):

1. Earth's surface and the sealed Garden of Eden

2. Chambers of the righteous

3. Chambers of the martyrs

4. Chambers of the wicked

5. Prison of the Watchers (Tartaros / Gehenna)

6. The Lake of Fire (lower hell, final destiny for rebel heavenly beings)

1.11 – LAYER 1: THE EARTH'S SURFACE AND THE GARDEN OF EDEN

On the top, we have the earth's surface. Eden is a real place on earth, created on the third day and later sealed.

Bereshith 3:24 — "So He drove out the man; and He placed at the east of the garden of Eden kerub, and a flaming sword... to guard the way of the tree of life."

Eden is on earth, not in the third heaven. It was sealed, not erased. Its vertical alignment is above the chambers of the just.

1.12 – LAYER 2: CHAMBERS OF THE RIGHTEOUS (BOSOM OF ABRAHAM)

Below the Garden, we find the chambers of the just. When a just person dies, they go to this chamber to sleep until the day of judgment.

Luke 16:22 — "And it came to pass, that the beggar died, and was carried by the angels into Abraham's bosom."

This is a place of comfort, not torment; below, in the realm of Sheol, but separated from the wicked; a chamber prepared for those who died in faith.

1.13 – LAYER 3: CHAMBERS OF THE MARTYRS

One level below, we find the chambers of the martyrs — those who died specifically for the sake of Yahuah and His testimony.

1 Enoch 22:5–7 describes a separate chamber for those "who were slain in the days of the sinners," waiting until the day of their vindication.

Revelation 6:9–11 reveals the souls under the altar who were slain for the word of Elohim and the testimony they held. They cry out for justice, they are given white robes, and they wait a little season until the full number of martyrs is complete. This corresponds to the martyrs' chamber.

1.14 – LAYER 4: CHAMBERS OF THE WICKED

One layer below them are the chambers of the wicked. When a wicked person dies, they also go to Sheol, but to a place of separation from the righteous and waiting for the final judgment.

Luke 16:23 — "And in Sheol he lifted up his eyes, being in torments, and sees Abraham afar off, and Lazarus in his bosom."

Notice: they are in the same underworld region (he "lifts his eyes"), there is a great gulf fixed (v.26), and he is not in the Lake of Fire, but in Sheol's chamber of the wicked. That is why, in the parable of the rich man and Lazarus, the rich (the wicked) lifted his eyes.

1.15 – LAYER 5: PRISON OF THE WATCHERS (GEHENNA / TARTAROS / "HELL")

One layer deeper is the prison of the Watcher angels, also called Gehenna, Tartaros, and the "prison" of the angels. This is what most people commonly call "hell," but biblically this is a specific department for fallen angels and many demons, not the final Lake of Fire.

1 Enoch 10:11–13 — the Watchers are bound until the great day of judgment.

2 Peter 2:4 — Elohiym cast the angels that sinned into tartaróo.

Jude 6 — the angels who kept not their first estate are reserved in everlasting chains.

The Watchers and 90% of the demons are located in this prison. This level is for heavenly beings that rebelled and their dead sons (demons), not for common human souls.

1.16 – LAYER 6: THE LAKE OF FIRE (LOWER HELL, FINAL DEPTH)

At the very last and deepest layer inside the earth is the Lake of Fire, the lower hell. This place still awaits its full opening at the end of times.

Revelation 20:14–15 — "And death and Sheol were cast into the lake of fire. This is the second death, the lake of fire."

Originally, the Lake of Fire was prepared for heavenly rebels.

Matthew 25:41 — "...everlasting fire, prepared for the devil and his angels."

This place is reserved for eternal beings that have led astray from

Yahuah, NOT HUMANS. The focus and original purpose of this place is the eternal punishment of rebellious spiritual beings — especially the Watchers and the devil.

1.17 – WHY YAHUAH PREPARED THESE CHAMBERS FROM THE BEGINNING

Yahuah is the perfect Architect. He prepared all these chambers from the beginning as part of His plan of salvation. If the Lamb was foreordained before the foundation of the world:

1 Peter 1:20

"Who truly was forseen before the foundation of the world, but was manifest in these last times for you"

Then the places of waiting (for righteous, martyrs, wicked), the prison of the Watchers, and the Lake of Fire also had to be prepared beforehand, to fulfill judgment, mercy, and final restoration. So from the beginning the just had a place to sleep in peace, the martyrs had a place to wait for vindication, the wicked had a place to await resurrection and judgment, the Watchers had a place of chains in darkness, and the Lake of Fire was reserved for eternal beings in rebellion. Nothing is accidental. Even Sheol reflects the perfect order of Yahuah.

1.18 – WHY YAHUSHA DESCENDED INTO SHEOL (NOT "THE LAKE OF FIRE")

This is why, when Yahusha died, He did not go to the Lake of Fire or to the final tormenting place, but to Sheol — the whole realm of the dead.

Ephesians 4:9

H"He also descended first into the lower parts of the earth."

Acts 2:31

"His soul was not left in Sheol, neither did His flesh see corruption."

He also proclaimed victory to the imprisoned spirits:

1 Peter 3:19

"By which also He went and preached unto the spirits in prison."

So He went into Sheol, not the Lake of Fire. He did not go as a tormented sinner, but as a victorious King. He confirmed Yahuah's justice in all the chambers. This corrects the traditional view that "He went to hell (Lake of Fire) to suffer." No. He descended to Sheol as Conqueror, not as a victim.

1.19 – ARCHITECTURE OF JUSTICE AND REDEMPTION

On Day 1, Yahuah created the abysses, created the darkness, established the foundations of Sheol, and prepared every inner-earth division needed for His righteous plan. So we can say that darkness was created so that Light would be revealed as supreme, abysses were created so that justice, waiting, and final judgment would have a place, and Sheol and its chambers were created so that every soul and every spiritual being would have its appointed destiny. Creation is not random. Even the invisible realms beneath our feet are part of Yahuah's perfect blueprint of salvation.

1.20 – WORK 6: CREATION OF THE DARKNESS

Jubilees 2:2 — "…and the darkness…"

Bereshith 1:2 confirms:

"And the earth was without form, and void; and darkness was upon the face of the deep (tehôm)."

1.21 – DARKNESS AS A CREATED CONDITION, NOT A RIVAL POWER

Darkness is not a force equal to light, evil by nature, Satanic, or chaos. Darkness is simply the absence of manifested light — the initial state waiting for Yahuah's glory to be revealed.

Yashayahu (Isaiah) 45:7

"I form the light, and create darkness..."

Tehillim (Psalm) 18:11

"He made darkness His secret place..."

In the plan of redemption light exposes darkness, light conquers darkness, and light reveals truth.

Yochonan (John) 1:5

"And the light shines in darkness; and the darkness comprehended it not."

Darkness exists to reveal the absolute supremacy of Light.

1.22 – WORK 7: CREATION OF EVENTIDE, NIGHT, LIGHT, DAWN, AND DAY

Jubilees 2:2 — "...eventide and night, and the light, dawn and day..."

This is the creation of time cycles.

Bereshith 1:5 parallels this:

"And the evening and the morning were the first day."

What Yahuah created here: eventide (evening twilight), night, uncreated Light (His radiance), dawn (morning twilight), and day. This is the origin of time, rhythm, seasons, prophetic cycles, Shabbat, appointed times (mo'edim), and the heavenly calendar. Before the sun, moon, or stars existed, Yahuah built the framework of time. There was light before the big luminaries were created.

1.23 – CREATION ACCORDING TO THE KNOWLEDGE OF HIS HEART

Jubilees 2:2 — "...which He has prepared in the knowledge of His heart."

This is one of the most powerful statements in all of Jubilees. It teaches that creation was not random, creation was not reactionary, creation was not experimental. Creation was intentional, crafted from Yahuah's own mind, will, and eternal plan. This means Eden was planned. Humanity was planned. Redemption was planned. Yahusha was planned. The Alef & Taw was planned. The bride of Messiah was planned. Humanity's destiny existed in the heart of Yahuah before Adam ever walked in the garden.

1.24 – FINAL SUMMARY OF DAY 1

The Seven Great Works (Jubilees 2:2–3)

1. Creation of the Heavens (Shamayim) — and Primordial Earth

2. Creation of the Waters

3. Creation of the Angels and All Spirits

4. Creation of Man's Spirit

5. Creation of the Abysses

6. Creation of the Darkness

7. Creation of the Light, Eventide, Night, Dawn, and Day (Time)

Day 1 is the foundation of the entire celestial realm — physical, spiritual, prophetic, and redemptive.

Chapter 2
The Great Work of the Firmament
Jubilees 2:4 and Bereshith 1:6–8

2.1 DAY 2 - WORK 8– THE ONLY WORK OF DAY 2: CREATION OF THE FIRMAMENT AND THE DIVISION OF THE WATERS

Jubilees 2:4

"And on the second day He created the firmament in the midst of the waters,

and the waters were divided on that day,

half of them went up above and half of them went down below the firmament

that was in the midst over the face of the whole earth.

And this was the only work Êlôhîym created on the second day."

Bereshith 1:6–7 (Dabar Yahuah – Yahuah Scriptures)

"And Êlôhîym said, 'Let there be a firmament in the midst of the waters, and let it divide the waters from the waters.'

And Êlôhîym made the firmament, and divided the waters which were under the firmament from the waters which were above the firmament: and it was so."

2.2 – WHAT IS THE FIRMAMENT? (RAQIA)

The Hebrew word used in Bereshith is raqia (עיקר), meaning: an expanse, a stretched-out structure, a fixed arch, a solid dome-like expanse, something beaten out or spread out like hammered metal. This is not empty space — it is a created structure with purpose, order, and spiritual significance.

In ancient Hebrew view:

The firmament is the divider between the heavenly waters and the earthly waters, the boundary of the visible sky, the foundation for the heavenly lights (Day 4), the "curtain" separating realms, the platform upon which the heavens are structured. It is both celestial and spiritual, physical yet symbolic.

2.3 – WHAT YAHUAH ACTUALLY DID ON DAY 2

Jubilees explains the process in detail — far more than Genesis:

A. He created the firmament "in the midst of the waters"

Before the firmament, everything was water. Creation was submerged in the primal deep.

B. He physically separated the waters

Jubilees says Yahuah divided the waters equally: half went above the firmament, half remained below the firmament. This explains why the heavens are often described as "the waters above."

C. The firmament covered "the face of the whole earth"

It was not a local event. It was global, stretching over the entire world.

D. This was the only work of Day 2

Day 1 had seven works. Day 2 had only one — but a monumental one. Yahuah created order, a boundary, and a celestial separation.

2.4 – WHY DID YAHUAH DIVIDE THE WATERS?

This division is one of the most symbolic events in all Scripture. It represents separation between realms: Heaven above, Earth below. Just as on Day 1 He separated light from darkness, now on

Day 2 He separates heaven from earth.

It represents the establishment of divine boundaries: no water above can descend unless Yahuah opens the windows of heaven (as in the Flood). No water below can rise unless Yahuah commands it. No human being can rise outside of firmament, but the only one who came from shamayin, Yahusha — other than that, NO ONE can ever step out of the earth. NO ONE, EVER.

It represents the creation of spiritual authority zones: above the firmament → heavenly realm; below the firmament → earthly realm.

It represents the prophetic blueprint of the Tabernacle: the firmament functions like a veil separating the Holy Place from the Most Set-Apart Place.

It represents the foundation for the prophetic times: on Day 4, the sun, moon, and stars will be set "in the firmament." Thus Day 2 prepares the stage for the heavenly calendar.

2.5 – THE SPIRITUAL SIGNIFICANCE OF THE FIRMAMENT

This act reveals many deep truths.

A. Heaven and Earth Are Not Equal Realms

Heaven is above → the realm of Yahuah, His throne, His malakim.

Earth is below → the realm given to mankind.

"The shamayim are the shamayim of Yahuah, but the earth He has given to the children of men."

— Tehillim 115:16

Some do not understand this reality and have been falsely taught of the false hope of man going to heaven, but I regret to inform you that no man can ever nor will ever go to heaven. The earth is for men and that is why that heaven will descent to earth for man to live with Yahuah forever, but the false notion of men going to heaven, has never been a biblical concept.

B. The Firmament Is a Witness

Like a covenant witness, it stands as a testimony of Yahuah's separation between what is holy and what is common, the divine realm and the earthly realm, the spiritual and the physical, the pure and the profane.

C. The Firmament Is a Barrier Against Chaos

Before creation was ordered, water symbolized chaos. By dividing it, Yahuah brought creation under complete control.

D. The Firmament Is the Pathway of Revelation

All visions of heaven in Scripture involve the opening of the firmament: Yachezqêl saw the heavens opened, Chănôk saw multiple heavens, Yôchânân saw the heavens opened, Yahusha ascended through the heavens. This shows that prophetic revelation comes through the boundary Yahuah established on Day 2.

2.6 – WHY DAY 2 HAS NO "AND IT WAS GOOD"

This is one of the mysteries of Bereshith.

Day 1 — "It was good"

Day 3 — "It was good" (twice!)

Day 4 — "It was good"

Day 5 — "It was good"

Day 6 — "It was very good"

But Day 2 has no such declaration. Why?

Because on Day 2 Yahuah created division, not completion. The firmament is a boundary — a separation — a veil. The work is good, holy, and perfect, but it is not a completed creation. Day 2 forms the structure (firmament), but Day 4 will fill it (luminaries).

Just as Adam formed on Day 6, Chawwâh completed on Day 6 after, Eden planted after Adam, etc. Yahuah forms → then fills. Day 2 is the forming stage, Day 4 is the filling stage.

2.7 – HOW DAY 2 PREPARES THE WAY FOR HUMANITY

Humanity cannot exist without atmosphere, regulated climate, protection from celestial forces, water cycles, boundaries between realms, separation between spiritual dimensions. The firmament is literally the protective architecture enabling human life.

It also establishes the principle that:

Man cannot break the boundaries Yahuah has set. Which becomes crucial when the Watchers descend in the days of Yarad — angels crossing boundaries they were never meant to cross. Breaking or crossing Yahuah's boundaries will always have huge consequences.

2.8 – THE FIRMAMENT AND THE PLAN OF REDEMPTION

The firmament embodies the entire Gospel pattern: a separation exists between heaven and earth, humanity cannot cross it, sin deepens the veil, Yahusha tears the veil, heaven becomes accessible again, restoration reunites what Day 2 separated. The tearing of the temple veil at the death of Yahusha is a direct reversal of Day 2's boundary for the redeemed.

2.9 — DAY 2 — Final Summary

The One Great Work: Creation of the Firmament and Separation of the Waters

1. Yahuah created the firmament (raqia) in the middle of the waters.

2. He divided the waters evenly: above and below.

3. He established heaven and earth as separate realms.

4. He created the celestial order that sustains life.

5. He formed the boundary between physical and spiritual dimensions.

6. He set the stage for the lights of Day 4.

7. This was the only work of Day 2 — forming, not filling.

Day 2 is the day of structure, boundary, separation, and preparation for the unfolding of creation and redemption.

Chapter 3
The Four Great Works of Creation
Jubilees 2:5–8 and Bereshith 1:9–13

3.1 – DAY 3 – INTRODUCTION: THE FOUR GREAT WORKS OF DAY 3

Jubilees 2:8 states clearly:
"These four great works Êlôhîym created on the third day."

These works are among the most foundational to the existence of life and the destiny of humanity.

3.2 – WORK 9: THE GATHERING OF THE WATERS INTO ONE PLACE

Jubilees 2:5

"He commanded the waters to pass from off the face of the whole earth into one place..."

Jubilees 2:6

"The waters... retired from off the face of the earth into one place outside of this firmament..."

Bereshith 1:9

"Let the waters under the shamayim be gathered together into one place..."

A. What This Means

Before Day 3, the entire earth was submerged. The waters covered everything — a global ocean, a world without visible land. Yahuah then issued a command, not a suggestion: the waters move, the waters withdraw, the waters retreat, the waters obey. This is the first time creation moves in obedience to His voice.

B. The Waters Gather "Outside the Firmament" — What Does This Mean?

Jubilees reveals something Bereshith only hints at: the waters receded to their assigned reservoirs, in places outside the atmosphere of the firmament, in the depths, trenches, and outer boundaries Yahuah established. This means the oceans, the deep reservoirs, the subterranean fountains, the great abysses were all placed exactly where Yahuah predetermined. This is why ancient cultures speak of the "waters below the earth" — Môsheh confirms this in the Torah.

C. Prophetic Meaning

The gathering of the waters reveals that Yahuah commands the forces of nature. Nothing is chaotic. Nothing is accidental. The sea does not stay in place by geological chance — it stays because Yahuah commanded it. He sets boundaries that cannot be crossed. Just as boundaries were set between heaven and earth on Day 2, boundaries are now set between land and sea on Day 3. This foreshadows the spiritual boundaries of righteousness vs wickedness. Yahuah also prepares the world for habitation. Land must emerge before vegetation, animals, mankind, nations, and Eden. Day 3 is the beginning of human destiny.

3.3 – WORK 10: THE MIST / DEW

Before vegetation could appear on the earth, Yahuah established a system of moisture that would sustain the land before rain existed. This divine mist or dew rose from the ground, preparing the soil for life. This work corresponds to the atmospheric and hydrological balance necessary for ecosystems.

Bereshith 2:5–6 describes this reality:

"...for Yahuah Elohim had not caused it to rain upon the earth...

But there went up a mist from the earth, and watered the whole face of the ground."

This mist is a sustaining provision, a life-giving system, a silent, invisible blessing, a sign that creation was being prepared from the inside out. Before man ever touched the soil, Yahuah Himself watered it.

Mist/Dew represents dependence (life flows from Yahuah), renewal (morning dew symbolizes mercy), and preparation (the earth is made ready before the seed appears). Dew is the first "irrigation system" of the world. It sets the stage for the next Work.

3.4 – WORK 11: PLANTS – CREATION OF ALL VEGETATION

This is the climax of Day 3.

Jubilees 2:7 declares:

"...and the seed which is sown, and all sprouting things, and fruit bearing trees, and trees of the wood, and the garden of Eden in Eden, and all plants after their kind."

Bereshith 1:11–12 confirms:

"Let the earth bring forth grass... herb yielding seed... fruit tree yielding fruit after its kind..."

The earth, once shaped and watered, now becomes filled with life.

A. The Seed Which is Sown

Seed is the foundation of generational continuity — in every dimension: biological (life reproduces), agricultural (food systems begin), spiritual (the principle of sowing and reaping emerges), prophetic (everything Yahuah does begins as seed), redemptive (the promised Seed of the Woman). Before humanity appears, Yahuah plants seed in the soil, preparing the world with sustenance. Provision precedes purpose.

B. Sprouting Things

These are the first living plants emerging from the ground. The earth responds immediately to His voice. The soil is already prepared by the mist; now it releases the life hidden within it. Sprouting things represent responsiveness to Yahuah, the first visible signs of life on the land, and the principle of immediate obedience in nature. Nothing delays. Creation responds perfectly.

C. Fruit-Bearing Trees

Trees are central to Scripture, shaping prophetic, symbolic, and redemptive themes: the Tree of Life, the Tree of the Knowledge of Good and Evil, the olive tree (anointing, covenant), palm trees (victory, righteousness), fig trees (Yasharal, spiritual discernment). Fruit symbolizes nourishment, abundance, blessing, righteousness. Where trees appear, culture, food systems, and symbolic revelation begin.

D. Trees of the Wood

Forests, timber trees, and structured ecosystems emerge. These are not only sources of food but also materials for building, habitats for future animals, stabilizers of climate and soil, and symbols of strength, order, and endurance. Yahuah fills the earth with a complete ecological architecture.

3.5 – WORK 12: THE GARDEN OF EDEN

E. The Garden of Eden

This is the first mention of Eden in Jubilees — and it reveals a critical truth: Yahuah planted Eden on Day 3, not after Day 6. This is a decisive revelation because it means Eden was planted before Adam, Eden was fully prepared, Eden was complete with rivers, beauty, and glory. Adam did not witness Eden's creation. He was placed into a garden already finished — a perfect picture of salvation: Yahuah prepares; man receives.

Eden is the first sanctuary, the first kingdom territory, the first expression of divine order on earth, the model for the New Jerusalem at the end of time.

F. Plants After Their Kind

Here begins the genetic law of reproduction: each species produces after its kind.

This law becomes central to the entire biblical narrative, especially in relation to the corruption of humanity by the Watchers, the hybrid nature of the Nephilim, the purity of the chosen seed, the meaning of holiness ("set apart"), the law of separation between kinds.

Creation itself testifies: Yahuah does not mix kinds — only the disobedient do.

This principle explains the judgments of the Flood, the separation of Yasharal, the genealogies, the warnings against mixture, the warfare in Canaan, the prophetic promise of a pure Messianic line.

Day 3 establishes the biological and spiritual order of purity.

3.6 – THE FOUR GREAT WORKS OF DAY 3 (SUMMARY)

THE FOUR GREAT WORKS OF DAY 3:

1. Gathering of the Waters into One Place

2. Mist / Dew

3. Creation of Vegetation

4. The Garden of Eden

Jubilees confirms:

"These four great works Êlôhîym created on the third day."

Day 3 is the day of foundations, ecosystems, provision, life, Eden, preparation for humanity. Yahuah is constructing the perfect home for His creation — a world fully ordered, provisioned, and sanctified.

Chapter 4

The Three Great Works of the Fourth Day

Jubilees 2:9–10 • Bereshith 1:14–19

4.1 – WORK 13: THE SUN APPOINTED AS A GREAT SIGN

DAY 4 — Jubilees 2:9

"And Elohim appointed the sun to be a great sign on the earth..."

Yôbêl 2:10 concludes:

"These three kinds He made on the fourth day."

On Day 4, Yahuah established three great works in the heavens.

We will look at each one.

Genesis 1:14–16

"...for signs, and for seasons, and for days, and years... the greater light to rule the day..."

4.2 – THE SUN IS A DIVINE APPOINTMENT, NOT JUST A LIGHT

Jubilees emphasizes what Genesis implies: the sun is appointed.

This means the sun has a divine role, functions as a celestial witness, governs earthly rhythms, and testifies of Yahuah's order. The sun is not an object of worship, as pagans made it. It is a servant, set in place to reveal Yahuah's will in time.

4.3 – THE SUN REGULATES SEVEN FOUNDATIONAL TIME CYCLES

Jubilees 2:9 assigns to the sun the government of:

1. Days

2. Shabbath (weekly cycles)

3. Months

4. Feasts (Mo'edim)

5. Years

6. Sabbatical Years

7. Jubilees

The sun is the divine clock of Yahuah.

It establishes the 24-hour cycle, the 7-day Shabbath cycle, the agricultural and sabbatical cycles, the Jubilee system, and the prophetic structure of history.

4.4 – THE SUN: SEPARATION AND PROSPERITY

Jubilees 2:10

"...and it divides the light from the darkness and for prosperity, that all things may prosper which shoot and grow on the earth."

Genesis 1:17–18

"...to rule over the day and over the night, and to divide the light from the darkness..."

4.5 – COMPLETING THE SEPARATION BEGUN ON

DAY 1

Day 1 — Light is created and separated from darkness.

Day 4 — The sun is appointed to visibly regulate that separation.

The Light of Day 1 was primordial, uncreated Light.

On Day 4, Yahuah assigns a physical bearer — the sun — to govern the cycle of light and darkness over the earth.

4.6 — The Sun as Engine of Prosperity

Jubilees reveals a dimension Genesis does not explicitly state: the sun was created "for prosperity, that all things may prosper which shoot and grow on the earth."

Through the ordered motion of the sun, crops sprout and mature, seasons follow predictable patterns, agriculture, food, and sustenance are sustained, and all life that "shoots and grows" depends on Yahuah's fixed order.

Day 3's vegetation was created in expectation of Day 4:

Yahuah formed → then filled.

Yahuah planted → then illuminated.

Yahuah prepared → then sustained.

Day 4 completes what Day 3 began.

4.7 – THE LIGHT OF YAHUSHA SETS THE BEGINNING OF EVERY DAY

The Light that appears on Day 1 is not only the first Light of creation — it is the Light that begins every single day from the foundation of the world to the very end of time. Before any sunrise, before any physical luminary appears, Yahusha Himself is the One who ignites the day. This Light is not symbolic. It is functional, celestial, and perpetual.

4.8 – YAHUSHA IS THE FIRST LIGHT OF EVERY DAY

From Day 1 to Day 3 the day begins with His Light, creation is ordered by His presence, and darkness flees before His radiance.

And this pattern does not stop after Day 4.

Even after the sun is appointed to govern daylight cycles, the true beginning of any day is determined by Yahusha's Light — not the sun; the sun is a servant; Yahusha is the source; the sun measures; Yahusha initiates; the sun rules the cycle; Yahusha defines the moment it begins.

4.9 – DAY BEGINS WHEN YAHUSHA'S LIGHT SHINES – NOT WHEN THE SUN RISES

This means the day begins with the Light of the Messiah, sunrise only reflects what Yahusha already initiated, the sun does not start the day, the sun manifests the Light already declared, and Yahusha's Light governs time before the sun imitates it.

Creation moves according to the Light of the Lamb.

This remains true in the final creation:

Revelation 22:5

"There will be no night there... for Yahuah Elohiym will give them light."

The Lamb's Light begins the eternal day, began the first day, and begins every day in between.

4.10 — The Sun Serves as Measurement, Not Origin

On Day 4, Yahuah appoints the sun to govern the day, mark time, measure seasons, and illustrate Yahusha's Light in the physical world. But the sun is never the origin of the day. It is the instrument that marks the rhythm which Yahusha Himself initiates.

The sun is the clock, but Yahusha is the One who starts the time.

This is why the Lamb is the Lamp in Revelation:

He sets the day, sustains the day, closes the day, and opens the next day.

He is the Alpha of every day and the Omega of every night.

4.11 – YAHUSHA'S DAY-BEGINNING LIGHT

"The Light revealed on Day 1 — Yahusha Himself — is the Light that begins every day of creation. Even after the sun was appointed on Day 4 to govern and measure daylight, the true beginning of the day is still set by the Light of Yahusha, not by the sun. The sun serves as a physical marker, but Yahusha is the One who ignites and initiates every day from the beginning of creation until the end. He is the first Light of every day, the source of time, and the One by whom the cycle of day and night is sustained."

4.12 – A CLEAR UNDERSTANDING OF BERĒŠHĪṮH (GENESIS) 1:5

Restoring the Biblical Meaning of "Day," "Evening," and "Morning"

Berēšhīṯh (Genesis) 1:5

"And ĔLÔHÎYM (אֱלֹהִים) called the light Day (yôm), and the darkness He called Night. And the evening (ereb) and the morning (bôqer) were the first day."

Most people quote this verse but do not examine the Hebrew. Here is the full restoration without altering any of your words:

4.13 – THE MEANING OF "DAY" – YÔM

Yôm means a full 24-hour cycle, composed of two equal halves:

12 hours of evening/night → roughly 6pm–6am

12 hours of morning/daylight → roughly 6am–6pm

Thus, yôm = a complete 24-hour day.

4.14 – THE MEANING OF "EVENING" – EREB

Ereb refers to the entire night cycle, approximately 6pm–6am, and includes dusk, evening, night, and the mingling of fading light.

It has two twilight points:

1. Around 5:59pm → beginning of night

2. Around 5:59am → end of night

Evening blends into morning because both belong to the same continuous cycle.

4.15 – THE MEANING OF "MORNING" – BÔQER

Bôqer marks the daytime cycle, approximately 6am–6pm, including dawn and morning.

It shares the same twilight transitions as ereb, proving they are complementary halves of one yôm.

4.16 – SCRIPTURAL PROGRESSION IN GENESIS 1:5

1. Day appears first:

"And Elohiym called the light Day (yôm)..."

2. Night appears second:

"...and the darkness He called Night."

3. Evening is mentioned as unfolding of night:

"And the evening (ereb)..."

4. Morning follows as the return of day:

"...and the morning (bôqer)..."

5. Together they form the day:

"...were the first day (yôm)."

Thus:

The biblical day begins with LIGHT, not with darkness.

4.17 – THE CORE POINT

Genesis 1:5 shows clearly:

The day begins with light, continues into night, and ends when morning returns the light again.

A full biblical day = 24 hours, evening + morning.

4.18 – WORK 14: THE MOON APPOINTED TO RULE AT NIGHT

Jubilees 2:9–10 • Genesis 1:14–16

The sun is the principal "great sign," the moon and stars are lights in the firmament, and together the luminaries govern light and darkness over the earth.

Genesis 1:16

"The greater light to rule the day, and the lesser light to rule the night: He made the stars also."

4.19 – THE MOON AND STARS JOIN THE SUN IN CELESTIAL SERVICE

Jubilees compresses the three luminaries into functional categories.

Together they regulate heavenly order, mark signs in the heavens, accompany the mo'edim as witnesses, participate in agricultural and seasonal cycles, determine day and night, and illuminate the firmament.

The sun is the primary ruler and timekeeper.

The moon and stars are secondary lights and signs, never independent clocks.

4.20 – WORK 15: THE STARS APPOINTED AS PROPHETIC WITNESSES

4.21 – THE STARS AS PROPHETIC WITNESSES

The stars are not random decorations.

Scripture describes them as the "host of shamayim," associated with the sons of Elohim (Job 38), and part of the signs in the heavens (Luke 21:25).

Day 4 creates a prophetic infrastructure in the sky — a visible testimony that time, history, and destiny are under Yahuah's control.

4.22 – THE MOON AND THE WARNING OF YAHUAH

(Why the Moon Was Never Appointed for Calendar Authority)

Although Yahuah created the moon as the "lesser light" to rule the night (Genesis 1:16), Jubilees makes a crucial distinction: the sun is appointed over the biblical calendar; the moon is never given authority over months, years, feasts, Shabbaths, sabbatical cycles, or jubilees.

4.23 – THE SUN ALONE APPOINTED OVER THE CALENDAR

Jubilees 2:9

"And Elohim appointed the sun to be a great sign... for days, for Shabbath, for months, for feasts, for years, for sabbatical years, for jubilees, and for all seasons of the years."

The text is explicit:

days, Shabbath, months, feasts, years, sabbatical years, jubilees, and all seasons are under the authority of the sun, not the moon.

4.24 – THE 364-DAY SOLAR YEAR WRITTEN ON HEAVENLY TABLETS

Jubilees 6:32

"Observe the years according to this reckoning—364 days..."

Yahuah ordains a 364-day year, 52 weeks, a fixed solar order.

This prevents displacement of feasts, shifting of Shabbaths, corruption of seasons.

Jubilees says this division is written on heavenly tablets so Yasharal will not forget the feasts (6:35).

4.25 – THE PROPHETIC WARNING AGAINST LUNAR OBSERVANCE

Jubilees 6:33–38 warns that if Yasharal adopts lunar observation, seasons will be disturbed, feasts will fall on wrong days, years will be dislodged, Shabbaths and festivals will be corrupted, and the holy will be mixed with the profane.

Jubilees 6:36 gives the core problem:

"They will make observations of the moon, how it... comes in from year to year ten days too soon."

A lunar year cannot align with the 364-day year.

The result: drifting feasts, misaligned Shabbaths, corrupted seasons.

Jubilees 6:38 concludes that whoever uses the moon for months, years, feasts, Shabbaths, jubilees "will go wrong as to the new months and seasons and Shabbath and festivals..."

4.26 – FINAL CONCLUSION ON THE MOON

The sun alone was appointed for the biblical calendar.

The moon is created for the night, for light, for beauty and praise (Psalm 148), but not for months, years, feasts, Shabbaths, jubilees, or seasons.

4.27 – THEOLOGICAL AND PROPHETIC SIGNIFICANCE OF DAY 4

1. Yahusha Foreshadowed in the Sun

Just as the sun gives light to the world, Yahusha declares: "I am the Light of the world." The sun is the physical symbol of the spiritual Light.

2. Day 4 Prepares Humanity for Covenant Worship

Without Shabbath cycles, feast cycles, yearly and jubilee cycles, Yasharal could not walk in the timing of Torah. Day 4 builds the framework for future covenant obedience.

3.Day 4 Establishes the Heavenly Calendar

The true biblical calendar is heavenly, structured by the sun as primary sign and the luminaries as witnesses.

4.Day 4 Completes What Day 1 Began

Day 1 → apparition of Light

Day 4 → appointment of light-bearers

Yahuah never leaves His patterns unfinished.

4.28 – DAY 4 FINAL SUMMARY

On the fourth day, Yahuah established the celestial clock, the prophetic calendar, the agricultural and prosperity cycles, the separation of light and darkness, and the framework for all appointed times and redemption history.

Day 4 is the day of order, governance, and divine timing—rooted in the sun appointed by Yahuah, with the moon and stars as supporting lights and witnesses, never as rival clocks.

Chapter 5
The Three Great Works of the Fifth Day

Yôbêl (Jubilees) 2:11–12 • Bereshith (Genesis) (1:20–23)

5.1 – DAY 5 – THE THREE GREAT WORKS OF THE FIFTH DAY

Yôbêl (Jubilees) 2:12 concludes:

"These three kinds He created on the fifth day."

On this day, Yahuah fills the realms of water and sky with living beings—the first nephesh chayah (living souls) of flesh and blood. Day 5 marks the beginning of moving, breathing life that swims, glides, and flies within creation.

5.2 – WORK 16: THE CREATION OF THE GREAT SEA MONSTERS

Yôbêl 2:11

"He created great sea monsters in the depths of the waters, for these were the first things of flesh that were created by His hands..."

Bereshith 1:21

"And Êlôhîym created the great sea creatures..."

A. THE "GREAT SEA MONSTERS" – TANNÎYN

The Hebrew word in Bereshith is תַּנִּינִם (tannîyn), meaning great serpents, powerful sea creatures, sea dragons, and deep-water monsters. Jubilees confirms them as "great sea monsters in the depths of the waters." They are not ordinary fish, but colossal beings, ancient aquatic animals, primal rulers of the deep, and the first fleshly creatures Yahuah made. They testify of Yahuah's power and majesty in the unseen places of creation.

B. "The First Things of Flesh Created by His Hands"

Before Day 5 there were no blood, no flesh, and no nephesh creatures—only land, seas, vegetation, and the ordered heavens. Day 5 introduces blood and circulation, movement and instinct, complex biological systems, and complete aquatic ecosystems. Life becomes animated for the first time in the history of creation.

C. Prophetic Meaning of the Sea Creatures

In Scripture, the sea often symbolizes the nations (Revelation 17:15), chaos and the unknown, and the deep mysteries of Yahuah. The great sea creatures proclaim Yahuah's mastery over the deep, His authority over visible and invisible powers, and His dominion in realms man cannot reach. Their existence declares: There is no realm—water, land, or sky—where Yahuah does not reign.

5.3 – WORK 17: ALL CREATURES THAT MOVE IN THE WATERS

Yôbêl 2:11

"...the fish and everything that moves in the waters..."

Bereshith 1:20

"Let the waters bring forth abundantly the moving creatures that have life..."

A. "Everything That Moves"

The Hebrew emphasizes abundance and motion. Day 5 includes schools of fish, crustaceans and mollusks, aquatic reptiles and amphibious creatures, microscopic life, river, lake, and ocean species, sea mammals, and deep-water crawlers. Every organism that swims, glides, creeps, or darts through the waters originates from this command. Yahuah fills the waters with overflowing life.

B. A Fully Designed Aquatic World

Day 5 establishes ecosystems and food chains, migration and navigation patterns, instinctual programming, reproductive cycles, and symbiotic relationships. Each species reproduces "after its kind," carrying the genetic code Yahuah designed.

C. Creation Obeys Instantly

As with the previous days: "And it was so." From shallow streams to the darkest abysses, the waters respond to Yahuah's word and burst with life.

5.4 – WORK 18: ALL FLYING CREATURES

Yôbêl 2:11

"...and everything that flies, the birds and all their kind."

Bereshith 1:21

"...and every winged fowl after its kind..."

A. A Sky Filled With Wings

The expression covers everything that flies: birds of every size and color; eagles, doves, sparrows, owls, and vultures; bats and gliding mammals; and flying insects. The Hebrew עוֹף (oph) includes any winged or airborne creature. The empty sky becomes a realm alive with motion and sound.

B. The Gift of Flight

Flight is a miracle of design—hollow, lightweight bones; intricate feather structures; wing geometry and aerodynamics; and internal navigation and migration instincts. All of this appears complete and fully functional from the first moment—no evolution, no randomness, no gradual development. Yahuah speaks, and the sky is instantly filled with fully formed creatures.

C. Prophetic Meaning

Birds often symbolize messages and swiftness, protection and covering, and vigilance and spiritual watchfulness. Yahusha uses birds to teach trust in Yahuah: "Consider the ravens..." (Luqas 12:24). Flying creatures silently preach that Yahuah provides.

5.5 – THE SUN RISES TO PROSPER ALL LIFE

Yôbêl 2:12

"And the sun rose above them to prosper them, and above everything that was on the earth, everything that shoots out of the earth, and all fruit-bearing trees, and all flesh."

This verse ties together Day 3 vegetation, Day 4 the sun's appointment, and Day 5 living creatures of water and sky. The sun "prospering them" means all life depends on Yahuah's appointed luminary; prosperity is built into creation by divine design; plant and animal life thrive under His ordered system. This is pre-corruption harmony—creation functioning exactly as Yahuah intended.

5.6 – THE THREE KINDS CREATED ON THE FIFTH DAY

The "three kinds" are the great sea monsters; everything that moves in the waters; and everything that flies—the birds and all their kind. Together they fill the waters and seas, rivers and streams, the sky above the land, and both visible coasts and hidden depths.

Day 5 is the day Yahuah fills the realms He formed earlier.

5.7 – THEOLOGICAL AND PROPHETIC SIGNIFICANCE OF DAY 5

1. Life Begins to Move

Days 1–4 created light, structure, and systems. Day 5 introduces nephesh life—creatures with motion, instinct, and interaction.

2. Yahuah Reveals Himself as the Source of All Life

No water system, ecosystem, or sunlight can create flesh by itself. Jubilees emphasizes that the first things of flesh were created by His hands.

3. Filling Follows Forming

Day 1 → Shâmayim

Day 2 → Waters divided

Day 3 → Land and vegetation

Day 4 → Lights appointed

Day 5 → Waters and sky filled

Day 6 → Land filled

Yahuah forms first, then fills.

4. The Sun's Appointment and Perfect Timing

The sun prospers the plants of Day 3, the creatures of Day 5, and the entire earth under its ordered cycles.

5. The First Blessing Over Living Creatures

In Bereshith 1:22, Yahuah blesses them: "Be fruitful and multiply." Multiplication is not human invention—it is built into creation by Yahuah's blessing.

5.8 – DAY 5 – FINAL SUMMARY

Day 5 marks the introduction of all fleshly life, the creation of the great sea monsters, the filling of the oceans with abundant creatures, the filling of the skies with flying beings, the beginning of biological reproduction, the prosperity of life under the appointed sun, and the visible harmony of creation under Yahuah's perfect design.

Day 5 is the day of life in motion—creatures that swim and fly—and the glory of Yahuah displayed in living beings inhabiting the realms He formed.

5.9 – THE TWO GREAT CREATURES OF YAHUAH'S CREATION

Liwyâthân (וְתִיוֹל) — Prince of the Deep

Zîyz (זִיז) — Roaming Winged and Field Beings

These two scriptural categories deepen the theology of Day 5.

I. LIWYÂTHÂN (וְתִיוֹל): THE GREAT SEA MONSTER OF YAHUAH

(Job 41)

A. A Creature Humanity Cannot Control

"Can you draw out Liwyâthân with a hook?" — Iyob 41:1

Implied answer: no.

No human can hook him, bind him, tame him, or subdue him. He is too powerful, too fearsome, and beyond human technology and strength. He stands as a primal sovereign of the waters, yet fully under Yahuah's command.

B. A True Day 5 Titan

In light of Yôbêl 2:11, Liwyâthân represents the earliest and greatest aquatic creations, the apex of deep-sea creatures, and a living monument to Yahuah's might.

C. Not a Mere Symbol or Ordinary Animal

Attempts to reduce Liwyâthân to crocodile, whale, or poetic metaphor do not fit Job 41's description of impenetrable scales, terrifying presence in the waters, and overwhelming strength. He is a real, pre-Flood aquatic titan, not a myth.

D. A Sign of Yahuah's Dominion Over the Deep

Job 41 is ultimately about Yahuah's sovereignty, not zoology. Humans cannot tame Liwyâthân, weapons cannot subdue him, armies cannot conquer him—yet Yahuah formed him.

Liwyâthân's existence proclaims: Yahuah alone rules the deep.

II. ZIYZ (זִיז): THE FOWLS AND ROAMING BEASTS OF THE OPEN FIELD

(Psalm 50:11)

Tehilliym 50:11

"I know all the fowls of the mountains: and the Zîyz of the field are Mine."

This verse combines "all the fowls of the mountains"—all flying creatures—and "the Ziyz of the field"—roaming, darting life in the open spaces.

A. Meaning of "Ziyz"

The root זִיז conveys moving thing, darting creature, roaming wild beast, and vigorous life in the open field. It is not a single species, but a broad class of wild birds, roaming field animals, migrating creatures, herd and open-range wildlife.

Ziyz captures the energy and abundance of Day 5 life at the edges of land and sky.

B. "The Fowls of the Mountains"

This phrase includes mountain birds, valley flyers, and sky-soaring species. It echoes Jubilees 2:11: "everything that flies, the birds and all their kind." The mountains and fields are alive because Yahuah filled the skies on Day 5.

C. "Are Mine" — Yahuah's Ownership

When Yahuah says, "the Ziyz of the field are Mine," He declares His ownership, omniscience, and sovereignty. All flying and roaming creatures trace back to His creative word on Day 5.

D. Ziyz as a Witness of Abundance

Linked to Bereshith 1:20: "Let the waters bring forth abundantly..." Ziyz embodies abundance, movement, multiplication, and diversity. These creatures become a legal witness in Psalm 50 that all creation belongs to Yahuah.

III. HOW LIWYÂTHÂN AND ZIYZ COMPLETE DAY 5

Together they display the full spectrum of Day 5: Liwyâthân represents the deep waters, hidden and fearsome realms; Ziyz represents the open fields and skies, visible and abundant realms. Combined with all fish and moving creatures in the waters and all birds and flying beings in the sky, Day 5 becomes a complete filling of the heights (birds and flying things), the depths (Liwyâthân and great sea monsters), and the open fields and edges of land (Ziyz and roaming life). Every realm Yahuah formed is now filled with vibrant, animated life that bears witness to His glory.

Chapter 6

The Creation of the Earthly Realms: Beasts, Cattle, Creeping Things, and the Primordial Behemoth

Bereshith (Genesis) 1:24–25, Yôbêl (Jubilees) 2, and Iyob (Job) 40

6.1 – DAY 6 – INTRODUCTION TO DAY 6

Day 6 marks the moment when Yahuah Êlôhîym fills the final empty realm of creation: the earth.

Days 1–5 established the foundations of existence: light and order, the separation of waters, vegetation and food systems, the sun, moon, and stars, and finally aquatic life and flying life.

Now Êlôhîym turns His attention to the ground, commanding it to bring forth beasts of the earth, cattle and livestock, creeping things, and the great primordial land-creature — Behemoth. Just as Day 5 introduced Leviathan as ruler of the waters, Day 6 opens with Behemoth, the colossal titan of the land.

Mankind will appear next — but that belongs to Part 2. This section focuses exclusively on all other land creatures.

6.2 – WORK 19 – THE CREATION OF THE LAND-TITAN: BEHEMOTH

(Primeval Counterpart of Leviathan)

Iyob (Job) 40 and the ancient traditions preserved in Jubilees reveal that Behemoth is part of the same primordial pair as

Leviathan. Leviathan is ruler of the waters (Day 5) and Behemoth is ruler of the earth (Day 6). Yahuah created both at the dawn of creation and separated them for the stability of the world. Thus Day 6 begins with the formation of this mighty creature.

A. "Behold now Behemoth, which I made with you"

Iyob 40:15

The phrase "with you" reveals that Behemoth is part of the ancient order of creation. He was created long before Job and is one of the earliest beasts of the earth, a real creature whose existence testifies of Yahuah's power. This wording refutes the idea that Behemoth is symbolic or mythological.

B. Behemoth, the Grass-Eater With Titanic Strength

Iyob 40:15–16

"He eats grass as an ox... his strength is in his loins, and his force is in the navel of his belly."

He is herbivorous yet possesses unmatched physical might. His immense power is concentrated in the loins, his colossal abdominal core supports overwhelming strength, his musculature and skeletal density are enormous, and his abilities extend far beyond those of normal animals.

C. "He moves his tail like a cedar"

Iyob 40:17

No modern animal has a tail resembling a cedar — enormous, rigid, and powerful. This eliminates interpretations pointing to hippos or elephants. It aligns perfectly with pre-Flood gigantism, Jubilees' record of ancient giants in both water and land, and Behemoth as the land-parallel to Leviathan.

D. "His bones are like bars of iron"

Iyob 40:18

"His bones are as strong pieces of brass; his bones are like bars of iron."

This describes a creature of extraordinary structure: impenetrable bone density, unmatched durability, towering pre-Flood size, and a body engineered for immense forces. Behemoth is the titan of the early earth — unmatched in strength and design.

6.3 – WORK 19 – YAHUAH CREATES THE BEASTS OF THE EARTH

Bereshith 1:24

After establishing the land-titan, Yahuah fills the earth with all other land creatures: lions, wolves, bears, elephants, deer, antelope, camels, all large mammals, all predators, and all land roamers. Each is created after its kind, with no mixing between genetic orders.

A. Wild Beasts and Predators

These creatures embody strength, territorial dominion, instinctual order, and ecological balance. Genesis and Jubilees portray them as fully formed — not evolving — with complete instinctual programming.

B. Herbivores and Grazers

These include antelope, buffalo, elk, deer, moose, and bison, all feeding on the vegetation established on Day 3.

6.4 – WORK 20 – YAHUAH CREATES THE CATTLE AND LIVESTOCK

These are the domesticable kinds, created before man but designed for his future stewardship: oxen, sheep, goats, camels, donkeys, horses, and bovines. They reflect Yahuah's provision, abundance, and intentional purpose. Their later roles — agriculture, transportation, sacrifice, covenant imagery, clothing, and food — will be addressed in Part 2 (Man).

6.5 – WORK 21 – YAHUAH CREATES THE CREEPING THINGS

Bereshith 1:24–25

Creeping things include insects, reptiles, amphibians, small mammals, burrowers, ground-dwellers, and crawling life. They occupy the low and hidden realms of the earth, serving critical ecological functions such as pollination, decomposition, soil aeration, and food chain equilibrium. Torah contains creation science long before biology named these systems.

6.6 – YAHUAH SEES THAT IT IS GOOD

Bereshith 1:25

Yahuah's declaration "It is good" affirms harmony, balance, order, purpose, and purity. No corruption exists at this stage. Predation is not yet violent — creation remains in perfect innocence.

6.7 – THE RETURN OF BEHEMOTH – THE CHIEF OF THE WAYS OF YAHUAH

Iyob 40:19

"He is the chief of the ways of Êlôhîym."

This means Behemoth is the greatest land-animal, the apex of creation's beasts, first in magnitude and strength, and a creature only Yahuah can approach. He is not merely included among other animals — he crowns them.

Just as the waters have Leviathan, the heavens have their hosts, the seas have their multitudes, and the land has its Behemoth, he stands as the earthly seal of Day 6 (Part 1), manifesting Yahuah's power, creativity, dominion, and authority.

6.8 – DAY 6 – FINAL SUMMARY

Day 6 (Part 1) includes the creation of Behemoth, the primordial titan of the land; the formation of all beasts of the earth; the creation of all grazing animals and livestock; the creation of all creeping and crawling things; the ecological structure of the land realm; the divine harmony of earth before corruption; and Behemoth as the opening and closing testimony of Yahuah's mastery.

Day 6 prepares the earth to be structured, filled, harmonized, vibrant, and fully alive. All realms are now complete — the heavens, seas, skies, fields, mountains, depths, plains, rivers, and land. Everything is ready for the final act of creation: mankind, covered in Day 6 — Part 2.

Chapter 7

The Creation of Man and Woman: Spirit Before Body, Body Before Union, Union in the Second Week

Bereshith (Genesis) 1–2 + Yôbêl (Jubilees) 2:14–16; 3:1–14

7.1 – DAY 6 – PART 2– INTRODUCTION – THE SPIRITS OF MAN AND WOMAN CREATED ON DAY 1

Yôbêl (Jubilees) 2 reveals that all spirits connected to creation were brought into existence on Day 1: angels, the spirits governing times and elements, the spirits of living creatures, and the spirits of man and woman.

Therefore, Adam's spirit existed from Day 1, Eve's spirit also existed from Day 1, and humanity began spiritually before humanity existed physically.

This explains Yahuah's statement:

"Let Us make man in Our image, after Our likeness." — Bereshith 1:26

The likeness (spiritual identity) already existed. Day 6 would give physical form to what had been created in the invisible realm.

Thus Day 1 is the origin of all spirits, and Day 6 is the embodiment of humanity.

7.2 – WORK 22 – THE FORMING OF ADAM FROM THE DUST

Bereshith 2:7

"And Yahuah Êlôhîym formed man of the dust of the ground, and breathed into his nostrils the breath of life; and man became a living soul."

At this moment, the spirit created on Day 1 enters the body formed on Day 6 through Yahuah's breath. Adam becomes a nephesh chay, a living soul — spirit and body united in a way no creature of Day 5 or Day 6 possesses.

7.3 – YAHUAH GRANTS DOMINION TO HUMANITY

Yôbêl 2:14

"A man and a woman He created them, and gave him dominion over all that is upon the earth..."

This reveals that Adam and Eve share the same purpose on Day 6, their destinies were established before Adam awoke, dominion is granted before their meeting, and both already exist in spirit.

Their dominion includes earth, sea, sky, beasts, cattle, creeping things, and every living creature. Humanity is appointed rulers under Yahuah — not participants in creation, but governors of it.

7.4 – THE DEEP SLEEP OF ADAM AND THE CREATION OF EVE

Yôbêl 3:5

"Yahuah our Êlôhîym caused a deep sleep to fall upon him... and He took one rib... and He built the woman."

This deep sleep is a divine operation. Yahuah builds the woman

(בָּנָה), a term of architectural design. Eve is fully created on Day 6. She becomes a living soul, a complete being, the physical embodiment of her spirit created on Day 1.

But here is the crucial reality: Adam does not see her, Adam does not know she exists, she is not brought to him, and they do not meet on Day 6. Genesis compresses events; Jubilees restores the true order.

7.5 – ADAM AWAKENS ON DAY 6 UNAWARE OF EVE'S EXISTENCE

When Adam awakens, he is alone. He believes he is the only human. He has no knowledge of Eve. Yahuah keeps her hidden.

Adam begins the rest of Day 6 without his companion.

Why? Because Yahuah is preparing him to learn solitude, to observe creation, to recognize companionship, to understand his need, and to be emotionally ready for Eve.

This explains Bereshith 2:20:

"but for Âdâm there was not found a help meet for him."

This refers not to Day 6 — but to the first week.

7.6 – THE FIRST WEEK: ADAM NAMES THE ANIMALS AND FEELS ALONE

This is the key detail: the naming of animals occurs after Eve is created, but before she is revealed. Adam sees the pairs among creation. He senses longing and incompleteness. He realizes he has no companion.

During this week Adam observes flocks and herds, sees birds and beasts in male–female pairs, and witnesses companionship throughout creation.

Thus Adam understands loneliness — not because Eve does not

exist, but because she has not yet been presented. This is divine teaching by experience.

7.7 – THE SECOND WEEK: EVE IS BROUGHT TO ADAM

Yôbêl 3:6

"...and He brought her to him..."

This event occurs at the start of the second week, not on Day 6.

At this moment Adam sees Eve for the first time. He recognizes her origin. He names her "iyshshah." He declares "bone of my bones, flesh of my flesh." The covenant of companionship begins. The union between man and woman is established.

Adam could not have said "now this is bone of my bones" unless he had lived long enough to feel the absence of companionship.

The delayed revelation produces longing, recognition, love, gratitude, and covenant meaning. Genesis gives the thematic summary; Jubilees gives the chronological detail.

7.8 – HUMANITY COMPLETES THE 22 KINDS

Yôbêl 2:15

"These four kinds He created on the sixth day... And there were altogether twenty-two kinds."

The four kinds of Day 6 are beasts of the earth, cattle, creeping things, and man and woman.

Humanity completes the 22 works of creation — corresponding to the 22 Hebrew letters, the 22 paths of divine order, and the 22 foundational creative acts. Man and woman are the crowning kind of creation.

7.9 – YAHUAH FINISHES ALL HIS WORK

Yôbêl 2:16

"And He finished all His work on the sixth day..."

This includes spirits created on Day 1, realms formed on Days 1–3, luminaries on Day 4, creatures on Days 5–6, Adam's physical body, Eve's physical body, the infusion of spirit into flesh, Adam's awakening, Eve's hidden preparation, the emotional shaping of Adam, and the future presentation that begins Week 2.

Creation is finished — but revelation unfolds in sequence.

7.10 – DAY 6 – PART 2 – FINAL SUMMARY

Day 6 (Part 2) establishes the divine order of humanity: the spirits of man and woman created on Day 1; Adam's body formed from dust on Day 6; Yahuah's breath making him a living soul; dominion over creation granted; Adam placed into deep sleep; Eve built from Adam's rib; Eve becoming a living being on the same day; Adam awakening but not seeing her; Eve remaining hidden during the first week; Adam naming the animals and feeling his solitude; at the start of Week 2, Yahuah bringing Eve to Adam; Adam recognizing, naming, and receiving her; humanity completing the 22 kinds; and all creation-work being finished.

This chapter restores the precise chronology given to Mosheh and preserved in Jubilees.

Chapter 8

Sanctification of the Shabbâth

Bereshith and Jubilees: Creation, Covenant, and the Rest of
Yahuah Bereshith 2:1–3 •
Yôbêl (Jubilees) 2:17–33

8.1 – DAY 7 – INTRODUCTION – THE COMPLETION OF CREATION

BERESHITH 2:1-2

"Thus the heavens and the earth were finished... And on the seventh day Êlôhîym ended His work which He had made, and He rested..."

Creation is not left open or unfinished. Bereshith testifies that the heavens and the earth were finished, that Êlôhîym ended His work, and that He then rested on the seventh day.

Yôbêl 2:23 adds a hidden layer:

"There were two and twenty heads of mankind from Âdâm to Yaăqôb, and two and twenty kinds of work were made until the seventh day; this is blessed and qâdôsh; and the former also is blessed and qâdôsh; and this one serves with that one for sanctification and blessing."

From this we learn that there are twenty-two heads of mankind from Adam to Ya'aqôb, and there are twenty-two kinds of work made until the seventh day. These twenty-two works and twenty-two heads are joined together for sanctification and blessing.

So Bereshith shows the completion of creation, and Jubilees reveals the numerical pattern and heavenly structure behind it.

The Seventh Day is not a day of forming or filling. It is the day of sanctification, blessing, and covenant. On this day, Yahuah takes what He has made and sets apart a day, a people, and a rhythm of time unto Himself.

8.2 – THE SHABBÂTH MADE A GREAT SIGN

Yôbêl 2:17

"And He gave us a great sign, the Shabbâth day, that we should work six days, but keep Shabbâth on the seventh day from all work."

Bereshith 2:3

"And Êlôhîym blessed the seventh day, and sanctified it..."

Together they reveal that Bereshith describes the blessing and sanctification of the day, while Jubilees explains that this day is a great sign. Shabbâth is not merely "a day of rest." It is the seal of creation, the sign that time belongs to Yahuah, and the marker that separates six days of work from the seventh day of qodesh.

From the beginning, time is divided, work is limited, and holiness is structured. Yahuah writes a sign into the weekly cycle — and that sign is the Shabbâth.

8.3 – SHABBÂTH OBSERVED IN HEAVEN BY TWO ORDERS OF ANGELS

Yôbêl 2:18

"And all the angels of the Presence, and all the angels of Sanctification, these two great classes, He has bidden us to keep the Shabbâth with Him in the shamayim and on earth."

Bereshith tells us Êlôhîym rested. Jubilees opens the heavenly scene.

In Heaven, the angels of the Presence stand before Yahuah and are throne-room messengers. The angels of Sanctification guard holiness and preside over qodesh times and spaces. These two great classes are specifically commanded to keep the Shabbâth with Him. This privilege is not given to all angels — only to these highest orders.

Even so on earth, this privilege will be given only to His set-apart people, not to all humanity. Thus Bereshith reveals that the Seventh Day is blessed and sanctified, while Jubilees reveals that it is actively kept in Heaven by the highest angelic orders.

Heaven keeps the rhythm of creation even before mankind is instructed. Shabbâth is first a heavenly practice, then a covenant gift.

8.4 – A PEOPLE SELECTED FROM THE EARTH TO KEEP SHABBÂTH

Yôbêl 2:19

"And He said unto us: Behold, I will separate unto Myself a people from among all the peoples, and these shall keep the Shabbâth day, and I will sanctify them unto Myself as My people, and will bless them; as I have sanctified the Shabbâth day and do sanctify it unto Myself, even so I will bless them, and they shall be My people and I will be their Êlôhîym."

Bereshith 2:3 tells us Êlôhîym sanctified the Shabbâth, but not who on earth would be entrusted to keep it. Jubilees reveals that Shabbâth is for a separated people and for a chosen covenant people, and that it is not given universally to all nations in the same way.

What Yahuah does to the day — He sanctifies it and He blesses it — He does to a people. He sanctifies them, He blesses them, He calls them "My people" and declares, "I will be their Êlôhîym."

The sanctified day becomes a covenant marker, and the covenant people mirror the day in sanctification.

8.5 – THE SEED OF YA'AQÔB CHOSEN AS FIRSTBORN OF SHABBÂTH

Yôbêl 2:20

"And I have chosen the seed of Yaăqôb from among all that I have seen, and have written him down as My first-born son, and have sanctified him unto Myself forever and ever; and I will teach them the Shabbâth day, that they may keep Shabbâth thereon from all work."

Bereshith establishes the day; Jubilees reveals who receives it. Ya'aqôb (Yasharal) is written as Yahuah's firstborn son. He and his seed are sanctified forever, and Yahuah Himself says: "I will teach them the Shabbâth day, that they may keep Shabbâth thereon from all work."

Shabbâth thus becomes a national identity, a covenant inheritance, and a sign of belonging to Yahuah. It is not discovered by human wisdom; it is taught by Yahuah to His firstborn nation.

8.6 – SHABBÂTH UNITES HEAVEN AND EARTH

Yôbêl 2:21

"And thus He created therein a sign in accordance with which they should keep Shabbâth with us on the seventh day, to eat and to drink, and to bless Him who has created all things as He has blessed and sanctified unto Himself a peculiar people above all peoples, and that they should keep Shabbâth together with us."

In Heaven, angels of the Presence and angels of Sanctification keep Shabbâth. On Earth, the covenant people of Ya'aqôb keep Shabbâth. All are called to keep Shabbâth together, to eat and to drink, and to bless Him who has created all things, as He has blessed and sanctified unto Himself a peculiar people above all peoples so that they should keep Shabbâth together with the heavenly hosts.

Shabbâth is the only day observed in the heavenly temple and in the earthly covenant community in the same pattern. The Seventh Day becomes the bridge between realms, the shared liturgy of Heaven and Yasharal.

8.7 – SHABBÂTH AS SWEET-SMELLING OBEDIENCE

Yôbêl 2:22

"And He caused His commands to ascend as a sweet savor acceptable before Him all the days."

Jubilees reveals that obedience to His commands — and especially the Shabbâth — ascends like a sweet savor before Him. Shabbâth is law, sign, and boundary, but it is also worship — a fragrance of obedience and love that delights Yahuah. Every generation that keeps Shabbâth faithfully becomes part of this continual fragrance before His throne.

8.8 – THE MYSTERY OF THE 22 HEADS AND 22 WORKS

Yôbêl 2:23–24

"There were two and twenty heads of mankind from Âdâm to Yaăqôb, and two and twenty kinds of work were made until the seventh day; this is blessed and qâdôsh; and the former also is blessed and qâdôsh; and this one serves with that one for sanctification and blessing.

And to this, Yaăqôb and his seed, it was granted that they should always be the blessed and qâdôsh of the first testimony and law, even as He had sanctified and blessed the Shabbâth day on the seventh day."

Earlier we saw this verse in the introduction; now its meaning unfolds. There are twenty-two kinds of work until the Seventh Day and twenty-two heads of mankind from Adam to Ya'aqôb. Both are blessed and qadosh and work together "for sanctification and blessing."

To Ya'aqôb and his seed it is granted that they should always be the blessed and qadosh of the first testimony and law, even as He had sanctified and blessed the Shabbâth day on the seventh day. The pattern is clear: the works of creation (twenty-two), the heads of mankind (twenty-two), the covenant people (Yasharal), and the covenant day (Shabbâth) are woven together into one structure of testimony, law, and blessing.

8.9 – SHABBÂTH, LAW, AND THE DEATH PENALTY

Yôbêl 2:25–27

"He created shamayim and earth and everything that He created in six days, and Êlôhîym made the seventh day qadosh, for all His works; therefore He commanded on its behalf that, whoever does any work thereon shall die, and that he who defiles it shall surely die...

Wherefore you do command the children of Yâshârêl to observe this day...

And whoever profanes it shall surely die, and whoever does thereon any work shall surely die eternally..."

Key truths emerge. The seventh day is qadosh for all His works. Whoever works on it or profanes it is under sentence of death. Shabbâth is tied to remaining in the land; violation brings being rooted out.

Because Shabbâth is the covenant sign, breaking it is covenant-breaking. Defiling it is like tearing off the seal that marks belonging to Yahuah.

8.10 – SHABBÂTH HOLIER THAN ANY JUBILEE OR FEAST

Yôbêl 2:30

"For that day is more qâdôsh and blessed than any jubilee day of the jubilees..."

Here Jubilees reveals the hierarchy of holiness. Shabbâth is more qadosh than all other mo'edim. Shabbâth is above sabbatical years. Shabbâth is above even Jubilee years.

It is the supreme holy day of creation, standing over annual feasts, seven-year cycles, and fifty-year cycles. Shabbâth is the master rhythm that defines all other sacred times.

8.11 – SHABBÂTH EXISTED IN HEAVEN BEFORE EARTH KNEW IT

Yôbêl 2:30

"...on this we kept Shabbâth in the shamayim before it was made known to any flesh to keep Shabbâth thereon on the earth."

Before any human was commanded to keep it, Shabbâth was already observed in Heaven. Therefore, Shabbâth is eternal, not temporary. It is part of Yahuah's own pattern, not merely human discipline. It is not invented; it is revealed.

Heaven kept Shabbâth before any man knew its name.

8.12 – SHABBÂTH NOT GIVEN TO ALL NATIONS

Yôbêl 2:31

"The Bârâ of all things blessed it, but He did not sanctify all peoples and nations to keep Shabbâth thereon, but Yâshârêl alone: Them alone He permitted to eat and drink and to keep Shabbâth thereon on the earth."

Jubilees is explicit: He did not sanctify all peoples and nations to keep Shabbâth thereon, but Yasharal alone. Them alone He permitted to eat and drink and to keep Shabbâth thereon on the earth.

So Shabbâth is a restricted holy privilege, a family sign, and a national inheritance. They are invited into the same rest and delight Heaven enjoys.

8.13 – THE SHABBÂTH LAWS ORIGINATE DIRECTLY FROM YAHUAH

Yôbêl 2:29

"Declare and say to the children of Yâshârêl the law of this day... that it is not lawful to do any work thereon which is unseemly, to do thereon their own pleasure, and that they should not prepare thereon anything to be eaten or drunk, and that it is not lawful to draw water, or bring in or take out thereon through their gates any burden, which they had not prepared for themselves on the sixth day... And they shall not bring in nor take out from house to house on that day..."

From this we learn: it is not lawful to do any work thereon which is unseemly; it is not lawful to do thereon their own pleasure (including sexual indulgence on Shabbâth); they should not prepare thereon anything to be eaten or drunk; it is not lawful to draw water; it is not lawful to bring in or take out through their gates any burden which they had not prepared for themselves on the sixth day; and they shall not bring in nor take out from house to house on that day.

These instructions anticipate and match Torah commandments in Exodus 16, 20, 31, 35, Yirmeyâhû 17, and Nechemyâhû 13. Jubilees preserves the heavenly origin of Shabbâth law, showing that these things did not begin at Sinai — they were rooted in Creation and then revealed to Yasharal.

8.14 – SHABBÂTH AS THE SUPREME BLESSED DAY OF CREATION

Yôbêl 2:32

"And the Bârâ of all things blessed this day which He had created for blessing and qôdesh and glory above all days."

Bereshith 2:3

"Êlôhîym blessed the seventh day, and sanctified it…"

Together they teach that the Seventh Day is blessed and sanctified, and that it was created specifically for blessing, qodesh, and glory above all days. No day stands above it. No feast surpasses it. No cycle replaces it. Shabbâth is the crown of the calendar.

8.15 – SHABBÂTH AS A LAW FOREVER

Yôbêl 2:33

"This law and testimony was given to the children of Yâshârêl as a law forever unto their generations."

The sanctified day in Bereshith becomes law, testimony, and everlasting statute for the children of Yasharal throughout their generations. Creation establishes the Shabbâth. Covenant preserves it. Heaven practices it. Yasharal inherits it. Eternity continues it.

8.16 – FINAL SUMMARY – THE SEVENTH DAY IN BOTH SCRIPTURES

Bereshith (Genesis) reveals that Yahuah finished creation, that He rested on the seventh day, that He blessed the Seventh Day, and that He sanctified it.

Yôbêl (Jubilees) reveals that Shabbâth is a great sign; that it is kept by angels of the Presence and Sanctification in Heaven; that it is given to the seed of Ya'aqôb on Earth; that it is holier than any Jubilee or feast; that it carries covenant penalties for defilement; that it is more qadosh than any other day; that it connects the twenty-two works of creation with the twenty-two heads of mankind up to Ya'aqôb; and that it is a law and testimony forever.

Together, Bereshith and Jubilees present the complete doctrine of the Shabbâth: eternal in Heaven, established at Creation, kept by the highest angels, given to Yasharal alone on Earth, law forever throughout their generations, sign of the covenant, holiest of all days, crown of creation and seal of the first week.

Chapter 9

The Perfect Work of Yahuah Êlôhîym — His 22 Works, His 7 Days, His Eternal Seal

9.1 – THE FOUNDATION OF ALL EXISTENCE

The Week of Creation is the foundation upon which all existence rests. It is the unveiling of the mind of Yahuah Êlôhîym expressed through time, space, matter, life, and spirit. In seven days — and in twenty-two works — Yahuah established all that is, all that lives, and all that will ever come to pass.

The heavens, the earth, the waters, the depths, the light, the luminaries, the creatures, the ecosystems, the prophetic cycles of time, and humanity itself were formed by His Word and for His purpose. Nothing appeared by chance. Nothing evolved through accident. Everything exists by divine design and intentionality.

9.2 – THE CREATION WEEK AS PROPHECY – EVERYTHING POINTS FORWARD

Creation is not only history — it is prophecy. Each day foreshadows the divine plan of redemption:

Day 1 → The Light of Yahusha revealed;

Day 2 → The separation of the holy and the profane;

Day 3 → Resurrection and new life;

Day 4 → The prophetic calendar of salvation;

Day 5 → Multiplication of life and movement of the Ruach;

Day 6 → The restored image of Êlôhîym in man;

Day 7 → The eternal rest of Yahuah with His people.

The Week of Creation is a prophetic map that anticipates the fall, the corruption of the two humanities, the need for redemption, the establishment of covenant, and the future restoration of all things.

9.3 – THE WORK IS PERFECT, THE PLAN IS ETERNAL

The Week of Creation is a heavenly blueprint, a structured revelation, a prophetic timetable, a covenant foundation, a celestial testimony, and a portrait of redemption. It stands as the prelude to the book's next great theme: the original humanity of Êlôhîym, the two lines of mankind, the intrusion of corruption, and the unfolding plan of Yahuah to restore His creation.

Creation proclaims: Yahuah is Êlôhîym.

History proclaims: His plan cannot be overturned.

Redemption proclaims: He will dwell again with His creation forever.

9.4 – THE CREATION WEEK – THE PERFECT BEGINNING OF THE STORY OF HUMANITY

Creation ends exactly as it began: with order, intention, and the sovereign wisdom of Yahuah Êlôhîym. Across twenty-two works and seven sacred days, Yahuah formed the structure of all existence — the framework into which the destiny of mankind will unfold.

Every boundary established, every realm separated, every cycle appointed was crafted with a single purpose: to prepare a world where humanity could walk with its Creator. Nothing was random. Nothing was chaotic. Nothing was accidental.

When the Seventh Day was sanctified, the first week became the eternal pattern for time, covenant, holiness, and destiny. But the story does not end with creation — creation is only the stage. The question that now rises — the question Book Two will answer — is this: What became of the humanity Yahuah formed?

For in the perfect world He made, something unimaginable entered. Something not formed by His hands. Something that would touch the heart of the first man and echo through every generation after him. Creation gives us the foundation. Humanity will reveal the conflict.

9.5 – FROM THE WORKS OF CREATION TO THE STORY OF HUMANKIND

Volume One has shown us the Light that precedes all things, the spirits created before flesh, the heavens stretched over the waters, the earth raised from the deep, the gardens prepared for life, the sun and moon appointed for prophecy, the creatures filling sea and sky, the beasts of the ancient world, mankind formed in the image of Êlôhîym, the woman fashioned in mystery, and the Shabbâth crowned as eternal sign.

Creation is complete. But completeness is not the end of the story — it is the beginning of responsibility. Because now that the heavens and the earth have been prepared... what will humanity do with them? Will they keep the order Yahuah established? Will they walk in the Light created on Day 1? Will they guard the harmony of the garden? Will they remain faithful to the covenant sign of the Seventh Day? Or will something disrupt the perfection of the first week?

Creation reveals who Yahuah is. History will reveal what mankind becomes.

9.6 – THE UNSPOKEN TENSION – THE TWO PATHS BEFORE MANKIND

Before the fall, before corruption, before the division of the two humanities... there was one humanity, created in purity, filled with purpose, crowned with dominion. But Scripture hints — even before Genesis 3 — that a choice stands before them: the path of obedience, rooted in the first week; the path of disobedience, rooted in another kingdom.

Book Two will open where Book One ends: at the moment humanity must choose which voice it will follow. Will Adam and his seed remain aligned with the 22 works of creation? Or will another influence — older than Eden, defiant since the beginning — enter the garden to challenge the order Yahuah established?

Creation prepared the world.

Now the world prepares humanity

BOOK 2
THE THREE HUMANITIES

The First Humanity and the Preservation of the Pure Line of Redemption

Introduction

From the Works of Creation to the Story of Humanity

HOW THE 22 DIVINE WORKS PREPARE THE FOUNDATION FOR THE FIRST HUMANITY

Book One unveiled one of the most forgotten and profound revelations of Scripture:

THE 22 WORKS OF CREATION.

These works—carefully ordered, precisely structured, and divinely executed—form the original blueprint of everything Yahuah intended for the world. They reveal:

how the heavens were arranged,

how the earth was formed,

how time, seasons, and order were established,

how light was distinguished from darkness,

how life was prepared before it appeared,

how every realm was completed before its inhabitants entered it.

Book One did not focus on humanity's failure, sin, or corruption.

It focused on Yahuah's perfect design.

It revealed the groundwork, the framework, the foundation,

and the original footprint upon which all human history would unfold. Now, Book Two begins the next phase of this revelation:

the story of humanity within that divinely prepared creation.

Where Book One showed what Yahuah made,

Book Two reveals whom He placed within it.

Where Book One established the structure of the world,

Book Two unveils the purpose of man within that structure.

Where Book One displayed the order of the works,

Book Two explores the order of human identity.

This volume begins with the first and most sacred stage of human existence:

Humanity as it was before corruption. The First Humanity.

Not fallen.

Not deceived.

Not broken.

But holy, instructed, clothed in light, and living in the presence of Yahuah.

This includes:

The First Seven Years in Eden

Adam's formation and instruction

Chawwâh's creation and presentation

Their union in the second week

The original state of humanity

The separation of light and darkness within human destiny

The foundation of the Three Humanities

The purpose of Book Two is simple yet profound:

To understand humanity as Yahuah created it—

so we may understand what Yahusha will ultimately restore.

Before sin entered the world, before deception, before judgment,

there existed a humanity that walked in perfect fellowship with its Creator.

This book restores that forgotten beginning.

It reveals the identity, purpose, and destiny of the First Humanity,

and sets the stage for the unfolding story of the Three Humanities

that continue throughout Scripture and prophecy.

From the 22 Works of Creation…

to the formation of Adam and Chawwâh (Eve)…

to the first seven uncorrupted years…

the journey of humanity begins here.

May this volume open your eyes to the beauty, order, and divine intention

of the humanity Yahuah formed in the beginning.

Chapter 1

The First Humanity: Qadosh From The Beginning

*The First Seven Years in Eden • The Two Kinds of Humanity •
The Origin of Disobedience • The Protection of Expulsion •
The Separation of Light and Darkness*

I.1 THE FIRST SEVEN YEARS IN EDEN

Humanity as It Was Before Corruption

Before the fall... before deception... before the expulsion from Eden... humanity lived through a period almost unknown in modern theology: The First Seven Years in Eden. These years are not a myth, nor a symbolic reconstruction. They are a literal historical reality preserved in Sefer Yôbêl (Jubilees) 3 — and they reveal the only uncorrupted version of humanity ever to walk the earth.

These seven pre-fall years are the blueprint of the redemption Yahuah will accomplish through Yahusha. Everything lost in these years will be restored in the Kingdom.

1.2 HUMANITY IN ITS ORIGINAL STATE

During these seven years, Adam and Chawwâh lived in a condition that no human after them has ever experienced. They were pure in heart and intention, instructed directly by Yahuah, free from death and sickness, free from corruption of body and soul, untouched by non-existent demonic influence, unexposed to angelic interference, innocent and without evil, clothed in the Light of Elohiym, and walking in uninterrupted fellowship.

This is not religious imagination — it is the original design.

Yahuah created humanity for light, not for darkness; for communion, not for alienation; for wisdom, not confusion; for obedience, not rebellion.

The First Humanity lived this reality in its fullness.

I.3 ADAM AND CHAWWÂH'S FIRST SEASONS: WHAT JUBILEES REVEALS

Jubilees 3 provides details rarely acknowledged in mainstream theology.

A. Adam was formed and instructed first

He was shaped by the hands of Elohiym, placed in the Garden, and taught directly by Yahuah Himself. Adam did not learn wisdom from angels, dreams, nature, or experience — but from the voice of Yahuah face to face. Berēshīth (Genesis) - 3:8 "And they heard the voice of YAHUAH (הוהי) ĔLÔHÎYM (מיהלא) walking in the garden in the cool of the day"

B. Chawwâh was created the same day — but not yet revealed to Adam

This detail is crucial to understanding the divine order. Creation of male and female occurred on the same day, but their union was delayed by divine instruction.

C. They were joined later, in the second week

Their marriage was neither immediate nor impulsive — it followed a period of formation, preparation, and sanctification. This shows a pattern still valid today: before union comes understanding; before covenant comes formation; before partnership comes identity in Yahuah.

D. Their early life was governed entirely by Yahuah's presence

There was no confusion, no temptation, no competing voices — only the pure teaching of their Creator. This was Eden in its original glory — and this is what Yahusha will restore.

I.4 WHY THE FIRST SEVEN YEARS MATTER

These seven years are not merely historical — they are prophetic. They reveal what humanity was before sin, what humanity will be after restoration, what Yahusha came to restore, what the Kingdom of Yahuah will look like, and what the redeemed humanity will become.

In Eden we see the First Humanity in its intended nature: pure, obedient, clothed in Light, governed by Yahuah's voice, free from corruption, and walking in harmony. This is the starting point for understanding the Two Humanities that emerge later — one that guards the light, and another that embraces the corruption.

The First Seven Years are the original testimony of divine order, sacred instruction, perfect fellowship, and unbroken obedience. Everything that follows in Scripture — from the fall to Babel, from Yasharal to the nations, from the prophets to Yahusha — flows from the disruption of these first holy years.

I.5 The Blueprint of Restoration in Yahusha

The most profound truth of this chapter is this: what Adam and Chawwâh lost, Yahusha came to restore. Yahusha is not restoring a broken humanity, a compromised nature, or a corrupted system. He is restoring the first image — the innocence, the light, the obedience, the fellowship, the purity of the First Seven Years of

Eden.

As it is written: "Behold, I make all things new." Not modern. Not altered. Not adapted. But new as they were in the beginning.

The First Humanity is the prophecy of the Last.

To understand the Three Humanities, we must begin where Scripture begins: a humanity formed by Yahuah's hands, instructed directly by His voice, clothed in His light, free from all corruption, destined to rule creation, and whose first years model the future Kingdom.

CHAPTER 1 ESTABLISHES THE CORRECTED THEOLOGICAL FOUNDATION:

Humanity was not created broken, sinful, or confused.

Humanity was created qadosh.

Only by restoring this truth can we understand the tragedy of the fall, the corruption of the Two Humanities, and the eternal restoration in Yahusha.

Chapter 2

The Two Kinds Of Humanity

Not Racial — But Spiritual

One of the most profound and misunderstood themes of Scripture is the reality that humanity is divided into two spiritual categories, originating not from race, geography, or culture, but from spiritual nature and divine order. This duality is not introduced in Eden, nor at the fall, nor with the murder of Qayin. It appears only when corruption enters the world through the fallen Watchers. To understand the redemptive plan of Yahuah across the ages, it is essential to understand how these two humanities emerge, how they function, and how Yahuah preserves salvation in each stage of history.

2.1 THE FIRST HUMANITY – THE RACE OF THE RUACH (SPIRIT)

Humanity in its original, uncorrupted state

The First Humanity begins with Adam — formed by Yahuah, animated by His breath, and clothed with His light. This original humanity was pure, uncorrupted, Spirit-led, taught directly by Yahuah, dominated by righteousness, walking in perfect fellowship, free from sickness, disease, and decay, free from angelic interference, free from demonic activity. Humanity reflected the order, purity, and intentional design established in the 22 Works of Creation.

This spiritual condition continued through the generations of

Adam, Seth, Enosh, Cainan, Mahalalel, and Yârêd. For nearly 1,200 years, humanity remained one unified spiritual group — the Race of the Ruach.

2.2 THE SECOND HUMANITY — THE RACE OF THE FLESH

A humanity formed only after corruption enters the world

Contrary to popular teaching, the Second Humanity did not begin with Adam's disobedience, nor with Qayin's murder, nor with the fall from Eden, nor with early human wickedness. The Second Humanity begins only after two major events: the Watchers abandon their heavenly nature, and the hybrid offspring are born.

This humanity is characterized by corrupted flesh, altered genetics, forbidden knowledge, sorcery, violence, spiritual oppression, social collapse, and the rise of the Nephilim and gibborim (mighty). Its emergence is not racial — it is spiritual and biological, rooted in angelic rebellion.

2.3 BEFORE CORRUPTION — HUMANITY REMAINED THE FIRST GROUP

Even after the fall, humanity was not yet corrupted

This truth has been nearly forgotten: humanity remained part of the First Humanity for almost 1,000 years after Eden. Even after gaining the knowledge of good and evil, they did not yet experience sickness, disease, genetic decay, demonic influence, spiritual contamination, angelic interference, or societal wickedness.

The only sins recorded before corruption were the disobedience in Eden and the murder committed by Qayin. Yet humanity's spiritual nature, physical purity, and divine blessing remained intact. They continued to worship in purity, live in extraordinary longevity, remain aligned with the Ruach, and preserve the identity given at the beginning. This period of preservation is part of Yahuah's redemptive mercy, keeping humanity pure until the appointed time.

2.4 THE DAYS OF YÂRÊD — THE TRUE SHIFT IN HUMANITY

When the Watchers changed their nature

Jubilees 4 and Enoch 6 teach that the Watchers descended righteously. Their mission was to teach humanity Yahuah's laws, and they served under divine instruction. Their descent was not corruption. Corruption begins centuries later — when the Watchers lusted after human women, abandoned their heavenly nature, entered into unlawful unions, and conceived hybrid offspring.

The Second Humanity begins only when their children are born. This moment marks the entrance of corrupted flesh, violence, sorcery, unclean knowledge, spiritual warfare, genetic corruption, and societal collapse.

From this moment forward, humanity becomes divided: the First Humanity — those who remain aligned with Yahuah; and the Second Humanity — those born from corruption and flesh. This division sets the stage for the rise of the Nephilim, the degeneration of the earth, the calling of Noah, and the plan of salvation.

2.5 THE REDEMPTIVE PLAN WITHIN THE TWO HUMANITIES

Yahuah's salvation blueprint woven into every stage

The purpose of the Two Humanities is not merely historical — it is redemptive. Yahuah reveals His salvation plan in every phase.

2.6 REDEMPTION IN THE FIRST HUMANITY – RESTORATION BEFORE CORRUPTION

The purity of the First Humanity is the prototype of what salvation will restore. Yahusha came not to create something new — but to restore the innocence, the light, the fellowship, and the glory that Adam carried before corruption entered.

2.7 REDEMPTION THROUGH PRESERVATION – BEFORE CORRUPTION BEGAN

For 1,200 years, Yahuah preserved humanity in purity: no corruption, no sickness, no genetic decay, no demonic activity, no spiritual distortion. This era of protection is redemptive mercy, showing Yahuah's desire that humanity remain pure.

2.8 REDEMPTION THROUGH SEPARATION – WHEN CORRUPTION APPEARS

When the Watchers corrupted themselves, Yahuah initiated a divine separation: the righteous from the corrupt, the pure from the hybrid, the obedient from the rebellious. Separation is not punishment — it is the preservation of salvation. Through this separation, Yahuah protected the line that would bring forth Noah, Shem, Abraham, and ultimately Yahusha.

2.9 REDEMPTION THROUGH JUDGMENT – CLEANSING THE EARTH

The Flood was not destruction only — it was the reset of humanity, preserving the First Humanity and eliminating the corrupted Second Humanity. Judgment is a redemptive cleansing, preparing the world for the next phase of salvation.

2.10 REDEMPTION THROUGH YAHUSHA – THE FINAL PURPOSE

The entire structure of the Two Humanities finds its fulfillment in Yahusha. He restores the purity of the First Humanity; He destroys the corruption of the Second Humanity; He becomes the model for the Third Humanity; He fulfills the plan written from the beginning. He completes every purpose revealed from Adam to Noah.

FINAL SUMMARY

From the earliest generations, Scripture reveals two spiritual humanities:

1. The First Humanity — Spirit-born, Spirit-led, Spirit-aligned

The image Yahusha came to restore.

2. The Second Humanity — Flesh-driven, corrupted, altered

The corruption Yahusha came to defeat.

And woven through both: Yahuah's Redemption at Every Stage

Preservation before corruption, separation during corruption, cleansing through judgment, covenant through Noah, fulfillment through Yahusha.

The Two Humanities are not a story of despair — they are a story of salvation unfolding through history, revealing the unbroken faithfulness of Yahuah to redeem His creation.

Chapter 3

The Origin Of Disobedience

Not Corruption — Simply the First Act of Breaking Yahuah's Command

One of the greatest misunderstandings in modern theology is the assumption that the event in the Garden of Eden introduced corruption, sinful nature, or moral decay into humanity. But the Scriptures teach no such thing — not in Bereshith (Genesis), not in Jubilees, not in any inspired text. Chawwâh's (Eve's) action was not the origin of corruption. It was the origin of disobedience. Disobedience is not corruption. Disobedience is not moral decay. Disobedience is not genetic alteration. Disobedience is not spiritual contamination. The first act of disobedience simply introduced violation of command, not transformation of nature. To understand this correctly, we begin with the two foundational truths.

3.1 THEY ALREADY KNEW GOOD LONG BEFORE THE FALL

Adam and Chawwâh did not discover goodness after eating from the Tree. They had lived in the atmosphere of goodness since the moment of their creation, because goodness is the nature of Yahuah. From the beginning, they lived in righteousness, purity, holiness, obedience, perfect alignment with Yahuah, the presence of the Ruach, and the goodness declared "very good" in Creation. The refrain of Bereshith 1 establishes this: "And Elohiym saw that it was GOOD." Everything in their environment — the world, their bodies, their minds, their fellowship — reflected divine goodness. So the problem was not that Adam and Chawwâh lacked knowledge of good. They were immersed in it. They were formed by it. They walked inside it. Goodness was all they knew.

3.2 WHAT THEY DID NOT KNOW WAS EVIL

Before eating from the Tree, Adam and Chawwâh had no awareness of the opposite of good. They did not know evil, rebellion, malice, corruption, spiritual wickedness, or deception. They did not know evil personally, conceptually, or experientially. When they ate of the Tree, they did not become evil, they did not become corrupted, they did not acquire a sinful nature, they did not receive an evil spirit, and they did not lose the divine image. They simply acquired something they did not possess before: awareness of the existence of evil. Not participation in evil. Not union with evil. Not transformation into evil. Only awareness.

This matches both Genesis and Jubilees: "Their eyes were opened." Eyes opened ≠ spirit corrupted. Eyes opened = moral awareness awakened. The text never says "Adam became wicked," "Adam turned corrupt," "Eve was filled with evil," or "Human nature became sinful." These statements do not exist in Scripture.

3.3 KNOWLEDGE ≠ CORRUPTION

This is the most important truth: evil did not enter them — awareness entered them. They gained information, not transformation. To claim that Adam became evil because he knew good and evil leads to a blasphemous conclusion: if knowing good and evil makes one evil, then Yahuah — who also knows good and evil — must also be evil. That is impossible.

Scripture says:

"Behold, Adam has become like one of Us — to know good and evil."

— Bereshith 3:22

Yahuah Himself declares that Adam became like Him in knowledge, not like Him in nature. The verse does not say that Adam became corrupt, that Adam became wicked, that Adam lost the image of Elohiym, or that Adam was spiritually damaged. The only transformation was intellectual: "to know good and evil." This is a change of awareness — not a change of essence.

3.4 WHY AWARENESS MATTERS IN THE STORY OF REDEMPTION

Awareness of evil does not equal participation in evil. Awareness does not pollute the soul. Awareness does not transform nature. Awareness does not corrupt the body. Awareness simply means that humans can now perceive moral contrast, distinguish wrong from right, recognize disobedience as a choice, and understand the concept of moral responsibility.

This is why they were still the First Humanity, they were still spiritually intact, they still lived long lives without disease, they still walked with Yahuah, they were still aligned with the Ruach, and they were still pure in body and nature. Awareness gave humanity moral self-consciousness, but no inherent corruption.

This distinction is foundational to the story of humanity — because corruption does not begin here. Corruption begins with the birth of the hybrid offspring in the days of Yârêd, over 1,000 years after the event in the Garden.

Thus, the disobedience in Eden is the beginning of awareness, moral choice, and accountability — but not the beginning of corruption.

Adam and Chawwâh already knew good, did not yet know evil, gained awareness not wickedness, gained understanding not corruption, remained spiritually pure, remained physically uncorrupted, remained aligned with Yahuah, and remained part of the First Humanity. Scripture is precise: their eyes were opened — not their spirit destroyed.

This chapter establishes the foundation for understanding how disobedience, awareness, and moral responsibility prepare the stage for the later corruption introduced by the Watchers — and ultimately for the plan of redemption that unfolds through the Three Humanities.

Chapter 4

The Half-Truth Of The Nachash

The Day You Eat of It, You Shall Surely Die — and How Yahuah Turned Even Judgment Into Redemption

The event in Eden is one of the most interpreted and misinterpreted moments in human history. Many believe that the declaration, "You will not surely die" (Bereshith 3:4), was a total lie from the Nachash (Gadre'el — the shining being, not a snake). But Scripture makes something clear: the Nachash spoke a half-truth, and Yahuah used this moment to reveal the first stage of His redemptive plan for humanity. To see this fully, we must weave together Bereshith (Genesis), Jubilees, and the prophetic meaning of "a day" in Yahuah's perspective.

4.1 WHAT THE NACHASH SAID WAS A HALF-TRUTH

The Nachash declared, "You shall not surely die" (Bereshith 3:4). He meant, "You won't die right now." And indeed, Adam and Chawwâh did not fall dead instantly, their spirits did not die, and they did not cease to exist. In this sense, what he said appeared true. But deception always mixes truth with falsehood. What the Nachash hid was the truth that mortality would begin, he concealed that the countdown to death would start instantly, and he obscured that the promise of death was literal — but in Yahuah's timeframe. This is why his statement was a half-truth — and the deadliest kind.

4.2 WHAT REALLY HAPPENED WHEN THEY ATE

Something irreversible occurred. Their bodies became mortal, their access to immortality was lost, their lifespan began counting down, physical death became certain, and humanity entered a new stage of history. Yet even this judgment contains the first traces of redemption. If Adam had remained immortal while disobedient, humanity would have lived eternally in rebellion — a condition beyond redemption. Mortality becomes a gift, not simply a punishment. It creates space for repentance, it limits the spread of corruption, it prevents eternal rebellion, it opens the path for resurrection, and it ensures Yahusha can redeem humanity later. Even in judgment, Yahuah is preparing salvation.

4.3 THE DIVINE MEASURE OF "A DAY"

Scripture tells us plainly how Yahuah counts time: "One day is with Yahuah as a thousand years" (2 Kepha / 2 Peter 3:8). Therefore, the warning, "In the day you eat of it you shall surely die" (Bereshith 2:17), means, "Within the thousand-year day, you will die." And this is exactly what happened. No human has ever reached 1,000 years, the full "Yahuah-day," because the decree of mortality stands from Eden forward. The longest lifespan in Scripture (Methushelach) ends at 969, still short of the divine measure. But concerning Adam — Jubilees gives us the precise, authoritative detail.

4.4 JUBILEES RECORDS ADAM'S DEATH WITH EXACT PRECISION

"And at the close of the nineteenth jubilee, in the seventh week in the sixth year thereof, Adam died... and he was the first to be buried in the earth" (Jubilees 4:29). Jubilees continues: "And he lacked seventy years of one thousand years; for one thousand years are as one day in the testimony of the heavens. Therefore it was written concerning the tree of knowledge: 'On the day that you eat thereof you shall die.' For this reason he did not complete the years of this day; for he died during it" (Jubilees 4:30). Adam lacked 70 years of the thousand-year day. He died at 930, paralleling Genesis. He died within the divine day, exactly as Yahuah warned. This proves that Yahuah's judgment was literal, the Nachash's assurance was deceptive, and mortality was the beginning of the redemptive plan.

4.5 THE REDEMPTION HIDDEN INSIDE JUDGMENT

Most people stop at "Adam died," but the purpose of this book is to reveal the redemptive plan of Yahuah in every stage. Here is the hidden truth: mortality itself was the first act of mercy. If Adam had remained immortal in disobedience, humanity would live eternally in sin, corruption would become permanent, rebellion would spread without limit, no resurrection would be needed, and no salvation would be possible. Instead, Yahuah gave humanity mortality so redemption would be possible, exile so corruption would not enter Eden, prophecy so hope would remain, and promise so Yahusha could come.

In Eden, the plan of redemption begins immediately. The moment man became mortal, the need for a Second Adam was set into motion. Mortality is not the end of the story — it is the doorway to resurrection. Without death, there can be no resurrection. Without resurrection, there can be no salvation. Without mortality, there can be no new creation. Thus, the death of Adam becomes the first prophetic sign of the coming of Yahusha, the resurrection of the righteous, the renewal of creation, and the restoration of the First Humanity. Yahuah always turns judgment into redemption.

The redemption thread becomes clear: the Nachash spoke a half-truth, Adam did die — but in Yahuah's thousand-year day,

Jubilees gives exact death details (4:29–30), mortality began immediately, and mortality is part of Yahuah's redemption plan. Because through mortality, corruption is limited, rebellion cannot become eternal, the Messiah can enter humanity, the resurrection becomes possible, and the First Humanity can be restored. The death of Adam is not the failure of creation — it is the beginning of salvation.

Chapter 5

"Like One Of Us": Knowledge, Not Corruption

How Awareness Changed Humanity — and How Yahuah's Redemption Was Already in Motion

Bereshith 3:22 is one of the most misinterpreted verses in Scripture. It has been used for centuries to teach ideas the Scriptures never claim: that Adam became wicked, that Adam became corrupt, that Adam lost the image of Elohiym, or that Adam inherited a sinful nature. But the text itself, when read through the restored Scriptures and the lens of Jubilees, teaches something profoundly different — something that reveals the early stages of Yahuah's redemption plan.

5.1 ADAM BECAME LIKE YAHUAH IN KNOWLEDGE – NOT IN CORRUPTION

"And Yahuah Elohiym said, Behold, Adam has become as one of Us, to know good and evil..." (Bereshith 3:22).

This verse clarifies one essential truth: Adam became like Yahuah in knowing, not like the Nachash in rebelling. Yahuah Himself defines what changed: knowledge, awareness, and understanding. He does not say that Adam became corrupt, became wicked, became sinful, or lost His image. The change was epistemological, not moral. It was knowledge, not nature; awareness, not corruption; understanding, not defilement.

And because Yahuah Himself knows good and evil — and remains perfectly holy — it is impossible to say that knowing good and evil makes a being evil. To claim that would mean that if knowing good and evil makes one evil, then Yahuah must also be evil — an impossible blasphemy. Thus, Adam did not become corrupt; Adam became aware.

5.2 WHAT CHANGED WAS HIS CONDITION – NOT HIS CREATED NATURE

Awareness awakened instantly, but corruption did not. After the disobedience, their eyes were opened, their awareness increased, their innocence ended, their mortality began, their environment changed, and their access to the Tree of Life was cut off. But their tzelem Elohiym — their divine image — remained completely intact.

Adam did not lose his spiritual identity, become sinful in nature, become morally decayed, become demonized, or become spiritually corrupt. None of this is recorded in Genesis, Jubilees, or any inspired text. Genesis and Jubilees portray Adam after the fall offering sacrifices, teaching his sons, walking with Yahuah, living in righteousness, and retaining the image of Elohiym. Adam sinned — but Adam did not become a creature of darkness. He remained the head of the First Humanity until his death.

5.3 DISOBEDIENCE BROUGHT CONSEQUENCES – NOT CORRUPTION

Yahuah's words were specific, and the results were precise: mortality, not wickedness; exile, not spiritual contamination; toil, not moral decay; awareness, not corruption; distance from Eden, not distance from Yahuah's presence. Adam's nature was not replaced; his environment was. Adam's essence was not destroyed; his access to immortality was. Adam did not lose the image; he lost the garden where that image was expressed in glory.

The origin of disobedience is not the origin of corruption. Adam and Chawwâh did not eat wickedness, did not receive corruption, and did not become spiritually twisted. They simply broke a command and experienced the consequences.

5.4 THE REDEMPTIVE PLAN: YAHUAH STEPPED IN IMMEDIATELY

The purpose of this book is to unveil Yahuah's redemption plan at every stage. And what we see in Chapter 5 is extraordinary. The moment Adam disobeyed, the plan of redemption activated — not centuries later, not with Noach, not with Abraham, not with Mosheh, and not only with Yahusha. Immediately.

5.5 REDEMPTION THROUGH PROTECTION

When Yahuah removed Adam from Eden, it was not punishment — it was protection. If Adam had eaten from the Tree of Life in a disobedient state, rebellion would have become eternal, corruption would have become immortal, salvation would have become impossible, and humanity would be trapped in disobedience forever. Therefore, Yahuah blocked the Tree not to banish man but to preserve man. Mortality is mercy. Exile is kindness. Boundaries are redemptive protection.

5.6 REDEMPTION THROUGH PROMISE

Right in the middle of judgment, Yahuah speaks the first prophecy: "The seed of the woman will crush the head of the Nachash" (Bereshith 3:15). Before Adam dies, before corruption appears, before the Watchers fall, before the Flood, before the covenant, before the Torah — Yahuah announces Yahusha. Redemption begins before history even continues.

5.7 REDEMPTION THROUGH CONTINUED FELLOWSHIP

After the fall, Yahuah speaks to Adam, hears Adam, teaches Adam, receives Adam's sacrifices, covers their nakedness, still blesses the family, and still guides the generations. Disobedience strained the environment — not the relationship. Yahuah did not abandon them — He drew closer.

5.8 REDEMPTION THROUGH LIMITING CORRUPTION

Yahuah set a boundary: no immortality in disobedience, no access to the Tree of Life, no eternal rebellion. These boundaries create the future space for the Flood, the covenant, the Torah, the prophets, Yahusha's incarnation, Yahusha's atonement, the resurrection, the Kingdom, and the New Creation. The entire plan begins here — with Yahuah preventing eternal corruption so He can one day restore eternal righteousness.

"Like One of Us": The Redemption Within Awareness

Adam became like Yahuah in knowledge, not like the Nachash in rebellion. Awareness awakened — corruption did not. Disobedience brought mortality, separation from Eden, boundaries, and awareness. But it also triggered the first movement of redemption: protection from eternal corruption, promise of the Messiah, preservation of the image of Elohiym, continued fellowship, limitation of rebellion, and the beginning of the redemptive blueprint.

Adam did not lose the image of Yahuah. He lost only the garden where that image shone perfectly. The plan of redemption was born in Eden — and it continues through every chapter of humanity's story.

Chapter 6

The Expulsion From Eden: The First Act Of Mercy

Not punishment — but protection and preparation for redemption

The expulsion from Eden has been misunderstood for thousands of years. To many, it appears as divine anger or punishment. But the Scriptures reveal it as something profoundly different: the first boundary of mercy, the first shield against eternal corruption, and the first action in the plan of redemption. Disobedience changed Adam and Chawwâh's condition, not their nature. What Yahuah does next is not retribution — it is salvation.

6.1 IF THEY ATE FROM THE TREE OF LIFE AFTER SIN – REDEMPTION WOULD BE IMPOSSIBLE

This is the theological core: if Adam and Chawwâh had stretched out their hand after disobedience and eaten from the Tree of Life, they would have become eternal beings, locked permanently into a fallen condition, incapable of repentance, unrecoverable, spiritually frozen forever, and immortal in rebellion. They would have become like the fallen angels: eternal, unredeemable, and unchangeable.

This is why Bereshith 3:22 is one of the most important verses in the entire Bible:

"and now, lest he put forth his hand, and take also of the tree of life, and eat, and live forever..." — Bereshith 3:22.

Living forever in a corrupted state, without death, without

resurrection, and without salvation would mean no redemption, no Messiah, no resurrection, no restoration, and no new creation. Immortality without righteousness is eternal destruction. Thus, Yahuah acted immediately.

6.2 YAHUAH REMOVED THEM AS AN ACT OF PROTECTION

The expulsion was not rejection. It was protection, preparation, and preservation. Yahuah removed them so that they could die physically — because mortality becomes the gateway to resurrection. He removed them so they could be redeemed spiritually — because death allows a redeemer to enter the story. He removed them so Messiah could come through their lineage — because if they became immortal sinners there would be no lineage for Yahusha to enter. He removed them so salvation could be offered to the world — because a dying world can be saved, while an immortal world cannot. He removed them so humanity could be restored rather than imprisoned — because exile prevents eternal imprisonment in rebellion.

Removing them from Eden protected them from eternal separation and preserved them for future redemption. Divine judgment was actually divine mercy in disguise.

6.3 THE EXPULSION WAS NOT THE GREATEST LOSS – IT WAS THE GREATEST GAIN IN HUMAN HISTORY

Every blessing of redemption that exists today flows directly from the expulsion. Because of their removal, death exists so resurrection can exist. Redemption becomes possible because mortals can be restored. Yahusha can come because humanity remained redeemable. Resurrection can be given because mortality opens the door to eternal life. Eternal life can be restored because immortality is now granted through Yahusha, not through natural access to the Tree.

If they had stayed in Eden and eaten from the Tree of Life, the universe would now be a place filled with eternal sinners, eternal rebellion, eternal corruption, no possibility of cleansing, no end to wickedness, no Messiah, no salvation, and no hope. Immortal rebellion is worse than death. Eternal corruption is worse than exile. The expulsion from Eden is not the "end of paradise." It is the beginning of redemption.

6.4 REDEMPTION BEGINS AT THE GATE OF EDEN

The expulsion from Eden was mercy, protection, preservation, preparation, and the first step toward Yahusha. If Adam and Chawwâh had remained in Eden and eaten from the Tree of Life, sin would be eternal, rebellion would be irreversible, humanity would be lost, Yahusha could never come, resurrection would be impossible, and salvation would not exist.

Therefore, removal from Eden is the first action Yahuah takes to ensure that a Redeemer can come, a new humanity can rise, a resurrection can occur, eternal life can be restored properly, and the plan of salvation can unfold. The first act after disobedience was not punishment — it was the beginning of the divine rescue mission.

Chapter 7

The Separation Of Light And Darkness Among Men

The Real Beginning of Corruption — and How Yahuah Intensified the Plan of Redemption

For nearly a millennium after Eden, humanity lived without corruption. Disobedience had occurred, but corruption had not yet appeared. Awareness had awakened, but the nature of humanity remained pure. This long period is often ignored in theology, yet it is essential: it reveals how Yahuah preserved humanity for redemption, and how humanity gently drifted toward vulnerability long before full corruption entered.

7.1 HUMANITY WALKED IN LIGHT – BUT THE FIRST SIGNS OF DECLINE APPEARED

Humanity did not become corrupt after Eden, but the Scriptures hint at the earliest signs of moral weakening: rivalry, jealousy, fear, shame, distance from Yahuah's immediacy, and weakening spiritual sensitivity. These early changes were internal, not corruptive. They affected behavior, not nature; they influenced relationships, not genetics; they distorted choices, not the human design.

This explains why humanity needed guidance, why altars began to appear, why sacrifices became necessary, and why Yahuah's voice had to intervene more often. Redemption begins here, as Yahuah compensates for this early drift. He teaches, He warns, He establishes altars and offerings, and He prepares righteous leaders such as Seth, Enosh, Mahalalel, and Jared. This was not corruption — it was fragility, and Yahuah responded with mercy.

7.2 THE FIRST HUMANITY – THE RACE OF THE RUACH (STRENGTHENED BY YAHUAH)

From Adam to Yârêd, humanity walked in righteousness, maintained purity, lived long unbroken lifespans, remained without sickness, heard Yahuah's voice, and experienced neither demonic activity nor angelic corruption. This era became the foundation of all future redemption, because Yahusha could only come through a pure human lineage. The Messiah needed an uncorrupted genealogy, and the First Humanity had to be preserved at all costs.

Thus, the First Humanity becomes the vessel of redemption, while the Second Humanity becomes the threat to redemption. Yahuah's purpose was not only to preserve purity but to preserve the lineage through which the Redeemer would come.

7.3 THE SECOND HUMANITY – THE RACE OF THE FLESH (TRUE CORRUPTION BEGINS)

This group did not appear in Eden. It appeared only when the Watchers, in the days of Yârêd, changed their nature, joined themselves to women, produced hybrid offspring (Nephilim), and introduced forbidden knowledge, war, and sorcery, causing genetic alteration and violence.

This is the real beginning of corruption — not the fall, not disobedience, not Qayin's murder, and not early human mistakes. Corruption begins with hybrid conception, not with Adam's disobedience. Impurity begins with angelic violation, not with human weakness. Darkness enters with illegitimate offspring, not with the Tree of Knowledge.

This is a new humanity — one Yahuah never created, never intended, and never blessed.

Redemptive insight: the moment this corruption appears, Yahuah's plan of salvation becomes urgent and visible, because the Messiah's lineage is endangered, creation is being rewritten, humanity is being distorted, the First Humanity is decreasing, and the Second Humanity is multiplying. The conflict is no longer philosophical — it is existential.

7.4 THE REAL BEGINNING OF LIGHT VS. DARKNESS

This is when the true division begins. The Line of Seth retreats to holiness, while the Line of Qayin mixes with angels and corruption. With this mixture, violence erupts, disease appears, war begins, sorcery spreads, bloodshed multiplies, the earth groans, and creation destabilizes. The world begins to shift from purity to chaos, not because of Adam — but because of the Watchers and their offspring.

Redemptive insight: Yahuah does not wait passively. He responds actively, raising prophets, empowering righteous men, warning the generations, calling His people to separate, preparing Noah, restricting lifespans, and judging the corrupt Watchers. Redemption is accelerating.

7.5 THE PLAN OF REDEMPTION INTENSIFIES

As corruption spreads, Yahuah begins Phase 2 of the redemptive plan.

First, He initiates the preservation of the pure lineage, placing a direct shield around the line leading to Noach. Second, He limits corruption: lifespans shorten, creation is restrained, and the spread of hybrid offspring is restricted. Third, He judges the Watchers: Enoch is sent to proclaim judgment, and the Watchers are sentenced. Fourth, He prepares Noach: the righteous remnant is trained, and the ark's blueprint becomes necessary. And fifth, He prepares covenant: the world is readied for a new beginning.

The redemptive plan is accelerating toward the Flood — not as destruction, but as cleansing to preserve the Redeemer's path.

A forward-moving, non-repetitive view emerges: humanity remained pure for nearly 1,000 years; disobedience did not equal corruption; the Watchers' union with women produced the true corruption; the separation between humanity begins in Yârêd's days; redemption begins as soon as Yahuah protects humanity; and the narrative moves from early moral drift, to spiritual separation, to internal conflict, to external corruption — all building toward Noach and the Flood.

Chapter 8

The Patriarchal Line Of The First Humanity

Adam → Seth → Enosh → Kenan → Mahalalel → Yarad → Chanok → Methushelach → Lamech → Noah

The Line Preserved for Redemption

The ten patriarchs of the First Humanity are not merely historical figures. They are the living architecture of Yahuah's redemption plan. Through them, Yahuah preserves the pure seed, establishes the lineage of the Messiah, maintains the Ruach-bearing humanity, sustains righteousness while corruption rises, and prepares the world for Noah's salvation event, the prototype of Yahusha. Each patriarch carries a unique element of the redemptive blueprint. Let us examine them one by one.

8.1 ADÂM – THE FIRST MAN, THE FIRST COVENANT-BEARER

The Beginning of Humanity and the First Revelation of Redemption

Bereshith 2:7

"Yahuah Elohiym formed man from the dust... and man became a living soul."

Role in Redemption

First to receive Torah directly from Yahuah, first to walk with Yahuah in purity, first to fall by disobedience, first to receive the prophecy of the Messiah.

Bereshith 3:15

"The seed of the woman shall crush the head of the nachash..."

This is the proto-evangelion—the first prophecy of Yahusha.

Legacy

Passed down the knowledge of Yahuah, taught commandments to his sons, maintained purity in the First Humanity for nearly a thousand years, and died at 930, lacking 70 years of the millennial day (Jubilees 4:30).

Redemptive Insight:

Through Adam's failure, Yahuah initiated the promise of a Redeemer.

8.2 SHÊTH (SETH) – THE APPOINTED SEED

The Restoration of the Righteous Line

Bereshith 4:25

"Elohiym has appointed me another seed instead of Hebel..."

Role in Redemption

Replaces murdered Abel as the pure lineage-bearer, restores the spiritual inheritance, and establishes the lineage of the Messiah.

- Legacy

Teacher of righteousness, his line is consistently contrasted with Qayin's corrupted line, and his name ("appointed") prophetically points to the Appointed Redeemer.

Redemptive Insight:

Through Seth, Yahuah restored what was lost, ensuring the

Messiah's line remained unbroken.

8.3 ENÔSH – THE MAN WHO RESTORED TRUE WORSHIP

Bereshith 4:26

"Then began men to call upon the Name of Yahuah."

Role in Redemption

Restored the sacred Name, reestablished prayer and sacrifice, and revived devotion and organized worship.

- Legacy

Sparked a spiritual awakening, re-centered humanity around Yahuah, and marked a turning point toward obedience.

Redemptive Insight:

Enosh initiates the first revival, preparing hearts for the coming generations of prophets.

8.4 QEYNÂN (KENAN) – THE PRESERVER OF ANCIENT TEACHINGS

- Role in Redemption

Preserved Adam's oral Torah, protected the pure teachings, and strengthened the foundations of righteousness.

- Legacy

Forefather of the prophetic line, kept the early world aligned with the knowledge of Yahuah.

Redemptive Insight:

Kenan safeguarded the doctrinal purity needed for the Messiah's genealogy.

8.5 MAHALALEL – THE ONE WHO "PRAISES EL"

Role in Redemption

Led a generation in worship, reinforced covenantal identity, and anchored the early assembly in praise.

- Legacy

Father of Yarad, filled his generation with reverence and honor toward Yahuah.

Redemptive Insight:

Praise preserved the spiritual environment necessary for the prophetic rise of Chanok.

8.6 YÂRÊD (JARED) – THE MAN OF DESCENT

His Lifetime Marks the Entrance of Heavenly Rebellion

Jubilees 4:15

The Watchers descended in the days of Yarad.

- Role in Redemption

His era marks the beginning of corruption on earth, the Watchers abandoned their heavenly nature, forbidden knowledge was introduced, and the Nephilim were conceived.

- Legacy

Preserved the pure line even as corruption grew and was father of

Chanok, through whom judgment and redemption were revealed.

Redemptive Insight:

Yared stands as the protector of the remnant, ensuring the pure lineage survives the world's first great crisis.

8.7 CHANÔK (ENOCH) – THE FIRST PROPHET, SCRIBE, AND TRANSLATED MAN

1. The Prophet Who Was Taken Alive Into Paradise

Bereshith 5:24

"Chanok walked with Elohiym... and Elohiym took him."

Jubilees 4:17–19

Chanok was described as the first prophet, the first scribe, the receiver of heavenly visions, the one who judged the Watchers, the man who was taken into the Garden of Eden, and the only patriarch of the First Humanity who did not taste death. He was not taken to "heaven" as later theological traditions claim. He was translated into Paradise, the restored Garden of Eden prepared for the righteous, where he still lives today, awaiting the time appointed by Yahuah. He is alive—not as a disembodied spirit in heaven, but as a preserved man in the place of life and holiness.

2. Chanok's Unique Place in Human History

Chanok occupies a unique position in the First Humanity. He walked so closely with Yahuah that he was removed from the realm of death. He is the first human to be taken alive into Paradise. He received revelations about the world that existed before him, the world he lived in, and the world to come. Through visions and revelations, Chanok saw the heavenly throne, the heavenly tablets, the judgment written against the Watchers, the timeline of history, the resurrection of the righteous, the final judgment of the wicked, and the renewal of creation. These were shown to him—not because he physically ascended into the third heaven, but because Yahuah revealed them to him while he was under the Ruach and later in Paradise.

Role in Redemption

3. He Revealed Coming Judgment and the Flood

Chanok was the first to proclaim judgment upon the Watchers, announce the coming Flood, warn of the consequences of corruption, and reveal that Yahuah would not allow the Second Humanity to reign forever. He prepared the way for Noah by making the coming judgment known long before it happened.

4. He Prophesied the Messiah and the Resurrection

Through visions, Chanok saw the Elect One / Son of Man, described His glory and authority, saw the resurrection of the righteous, and the final separation between the just and the wicked. He became one of the earliest prophetic voices pointing clearly to Yahusha and the final restoration.

5. He Became a Living Sign of the Future Redemption

Chanok's translation into Paradise is a sign that death is not the final destiny of the righteous, a prophetic shadow of the transformation Yahuah will grant to His people, and a living testimony that a human being can be preserved, body and spirit, by Yahuah's power. Just as Adam's death revealed the consequence of disobedience, Chanok's translation reveals the hope of the redeemed.

Chanok's Legacy

6. Father of Methushelach

He passes his prophetic knowledge to Methushelach. Through Methushelach, his teachings reach Lamech and Noah.

7. Guardian of the Prophetic Writings

Chanok wrote down what he saw and heard, recorded the history from creation to the final age, and documented the fall of the Watchers and the plan of redemption. His books were meant to preserve truth for future generations, expose the works of darkness, and reveal Yahuah's justice and mercy. Because his writings uncover the origin of evil, the corruption of angels, the truth of the Nephilim, and the full plan of redemption, the corrupted line of the Second Humanity worked to conceal them, to keep the world blind and far from the truth of Yahuah. Yet Yahuah preserved Chanok's testimony through faithful remnants, traditions, and later rediscoveries.

- Redemptive Insight

Chanok is the first man to walk so closely with Yahuah that death could not claim him, the first to be taken alive into Paradise, the first to see the complete map of redemption, from creation to the new age, and a constant reminder that Yahuah's plan is not just to forgive, but to preserve and transform. His life declares that humanity was not created for death. Humanity was created for fellowship, revelation, and life in the presence of Yahuah. Chanok's translation into Paradise points forward to the day when the redeemed will also be restored to a perfected creation, walking with Yahuah, not in heaven as disembodied spirits, but in a renewed earth under His eternal reign.

8.8 METHUSHELACH – THE MAN WHO HELD BACK JUDGMENT

The Longest Life Ever Lived, a Prophecy of Mercy

The meaning of his name is prophetic: "When he dies, it will be sent," meaning judgment would not fall until Methushelach's life ended. Yahuah tied the timing of the Flood to this man's lifespan, making him a living symbol of divine patience.

1. His Life Delayed the Flood for Centuries

Yahuah allowed Methushelach to live 969 years, longer than any other man, in order to delay destruction, extend mercy, give humanity time to repent, and preserve the pure line long enough for Noah to be born, raised, and prepared. Methushelach's lifespan is not random. It is deliberate, strategic, and filled with grace.

2. He Preserved Chanok's Teachings

As the son of Chanok, he guarded the first prophetic writings, protected the testimony of the Watchers' judgment, transmitted the teachings of righteousness to the next generation, and ensured that Lamech and Noah understood the coming crisis. Without Methushelach, the prophetic warnings might have vanished as corruption grew.

3. He Raised Lamech in Righteousness

Methushelach prepared his son Lamech to withstand the violence of the Nephilim, the corruption of the Watchers' knowledge, and the moral collapse of society.

- Legacy

969 years — the longest recorded lifespan. His longevity is not a curiosity; it is a timeline of mercy.

- Redemptive Insight

Methushelach's life demonstrates that Yahuah will delay judgment as long as righteousness remains on earth. Mercy always precedes wrath. Judgment falls only when every avenue of redemption has been exhausted. He is the living embodiment of "Yahuah is patient, not willing that any should perish." He stands as a prophetic monument to the kindness of Yahuah.

8.9 LAMECH – THE RIGHTEOUS FATHER OF NOAH

The Bridge Between Purity and Corruption

Bereshith 5:28–29

"This one shall comfort us concerning our work and toil..."

Lamech lived in the first generation where corruption became visible everywhere: the Nephilim walked the earth, violence covered cities and regions, the hybrid offspring dominated nations, and sorcery and bloodshed became normal. Yet Lamech remained righteous — a rare light in a darkening world.

1. He Recognized Noah's Divine Calling

Lamech saw prophetically that his son Noah would bring comfort, bring preservation, and bring salvation through the Flood. He prophetically announced: "This one shall comfort us..." (Bereshith 5:29). He was the first to reveal that Noah carried a redemptive destiny.

2. He Raised the Final Patriarch of the First Humanity

Lamech taught Noah the ways of righteousness, the teachings of Adam, Seth, Enosh, and Chanok, the dangers of corruption, and the judgment of the Watchers. He prepared Noah to stand alone in purity.

3. He Maintained Purity Amid Rising Corruption

Lamech witnessed the spread of hybrid bloodlines, the collapse of morality, the spread of forbidden knowledge, and the violence that filled the world. Despite living in the darkest generation before the Flood, Lamech preserved the holy tradition and ensured it reached Noah.

- Legacy

The spiritual bridge between the righteous ages and the age of corruption, a father whose righteousness helped shape the man who would save humanity.

Redemptive Insight

Lamech embodies the prophetic heartbeat of Yahuah's plan: before

Yahuah saves the world, He raises someone who understands the mission. Noah did not rise in a vacuum — Lamech laid the foundation.

8.10 NÔACH (NOAH) — THE LAST PURE MAN OF THE FIRST HUMANITY

The Chosen Vessel to Preserve Redemption Through the Waters of Judgment

Bereshith 6:9

"Noach was perfect in his generations and walked with Elohiym."

Jubilees 5:12

"Noach alone remained uncorrupted when the earth was filled with impurity."

Noah's "perfection" refers to purity of lineage (tamiym), not flawlessness of character. He was the last man whose genealogy had no corruption from the Watchers.

1. Chosen to Preserve the Pure Seed

Noah stands as the final representative of the First Humanity, carrying the untouched genetic legacy of Adam. Through Noah, Yahuah preserved the lineage of Messiah, prevented the total extinction of the Ruach-bearing humanity, and ensured the earth would not be lost to hybrid corruption.

2. Builder of the Ark

The Ark is the first great symbol of salvation, separation, covenant, and new creation. Noah built the vessel through which the righteous would be preserved, creation would be reset, and the promise of redemption would continue.

3. Preacher of Righteousness

For over a century, Noah warned the world to repent, to turn from corruption, and to prepare for judgment. He embodied Yahuah's patience and compassion.

4. Carrier of Covenant

After the Flood, Noah offered the first altar in the renewed world, received Yahuah's covenant, became the father of all nations, and carried the prophetic line into the post-Flood earth.

5. Prototype of Messiah — A Savior of His Generation

Noah saved humanity through water. Yahusha saves humanity through blood. The patterns align: Noah brought salvation to a remnant, Yahusha brings salvation to the world, Noah introduced a new creation, Yahusha brings the final new creation, Noah saved through an ark, Yahusha is the Ark of Salvation.

- Legacy

Preserved Adam's pure lineage, became the dividing line between the First and Second worlds, father of the new humanity, and carrier of the path that leads to Abraham and Yahusha.

- Redemptive Insight

Noah's story is the earliest, clearest prophecy of Yahusha's redemption: saved through water → saved through blood. Noah saved the first creation. Yahusha saves the final creation.

8.11 THE GENEALOGY OF REDEMPTION

These ten patriarchs are the guardians of the pure seed, the carriers of the Ruach, the protectors of the Messiah's lineage, the prophetic timeline from Eden to the Flood, and the framework upon which Yahusha's incarnation is built. Every name, every generation, every life is part of Yahuah's unbroken plan: from Adam → to Noah → to Abraham → to David → to Yahusha. The First Humanity preserved the world long enough for the Redeemer to eventually come.

Chapter 9

The Purity Of The First Humanity Before The Flood

The Race of the Ruach — The Image of Elohiym Preserved on Earth

Before corruption entered the world, before the Watchers fell, before Nephilim walked the earth, there existed an age unlike any other: The Age of the First Humanity. This humanity—from Adam to Noah—was the only generation in world history that lived without spiritual enemies, without genetic corruption, without demonic interference, without sickness or decay, without forbidden knowledge, and without the presence of evil beings in their environment. They were the pure blueprint of what Yahuah intended humanity to be. And for 1,200 years, Yahuah protected their purity because their existence was crucial for His unfolding plan of redemption. This chapter explores what made this First Humanity unique by unveiling their spiritual identity, their societal purity, and their role in Yahuah's eternal purpose.

9.1 THEY CARRIED THE RUACH OF ELOHIYM – THE INNER DESIGN OF THE FIRST HUMANITY

Bereshith 2:7

"Yahuah Elohiym breathed... and man became a living soul."

The First Humanity did not merely live — they lived from within the Ruach. Their spirit enabled them to hear Yahuah clearly, discern truth effortlessly, walk in righteousness naturally, and receive revelation without distortion. This was not "religion." It was direct correspondence with their Maker, the normal mode of life for the First Humanity.

Redemptive Insight

Yahusha came to restore this Ruach-bearing identity, not create something new. The First Humanity reveals the original destiny Yahusha came to redeem.

9.2 THEIR SPIRITUAL GENETICS ALLOWED PERFECT FELLOWSHIP WITH YAHUAH

What made them unique was not only their spirit but their whole constitution: unbroken DNA, uncorrupted mind, unpolluted environment, untainted bloodline, and clarity of soul and body. They possessed a physical and spiritual design that no later generation would ever inherit naturally. There were no spiritual blockages, no generational corruption, no inherited evil, no demonic influence. This humanity lived in a world where heaven and earth touched without interference.

Redemptive Insight

Yahuah preserved this pure design for 1,200 years to ensure the Redeemer's lineage would remain free from corruption until the appointed time.

9.3 THEIR WORLD WAS PEACEFUL AND UNBROKEN

The First Humanity lived in peace, unity, moral clarity, harmony with creation, and spiritual awareness. The only sins recorded were the disobedience of Adam and Chawwâh and the murder by Qayin. Neither of these events introduced spiritual corruption into the world system. Their world did not yet know vice, sorcery, war, genetic alteration, demonic oppression, or supernatural hostility. This was not "innocence"—it was purity in knowledge and purity in environment.

Redemptive Insight

The peace of the First Humanity serves as a prophetic preview of the New Creation, when Yahusha restores the world to the purity that existed before corruption.

9.4 THEY WALKED WITH ELOHIYM WITH PERSONAL ACCESS AND CLEAR COMMUNICATION

Bereshith 3:8

"Yahuah Elohiym walking in the garden..."

This was not mythology. It was the lifestyle of the First Humanity: direct encounters, audible communication, open fellowship. Even after Eden, the pattern continued. Adam taught commandments. Seth reestablished purity. Enosh led the first organized worship. Chanok walked with Elohiym and was taken to Paradise. Noah received detailed divine instructions. The line remained covenantal, prophetic, and deeply spiritual.

Redemptive Insight

This direct communion prefigures Yahusha's role as the mediator restoring access to Yahuah.

9.5 THEY PRESERVED THE TRUE KNOWLEDGE OF YAHUAH – THE ORAL TORAH OF EDEN

The First Humanity preserved the Name of Yahuah, the heavenly calendar, the original commandments, the laws of purity and sacrifice, the understanding of creation, the prophetic traditions, and the covenantal identity. From Adam to Noah, this knowledge remained unbroken. But Yahuah did more: He sent righteous Watchers to teach humanity, not fallen angels — holy ones, as Jubilees and Chanok reveal. Their purpose was to instruct in righteousness, establish justice, reveal the heavenly order, and assist the pure humanity. For 700 years, earth enjoyed a combined ministry of patriarchs on earth and Watchers from heaven. This era was a spiritual golden age.

Redemptive Insight

Before judgment, Yahuah always gives instruction. The Watchers' original mission mirrors Yahusha's teaching ministry.

9.6 PURITY WAS PRESERVED BECAUSE THERE WERE NO SPIRITUAL ENEMIES – UNTIL THE WATCHERS FELL

A major misconception must be corrected: the Watchers' arrival was not the beginning of corruption. Their arrival marked the height of teaching and righteousness. Corruption began only when they abandoned their heavenly assignment around year 1200. When they took human women, broke their oaths, introduced forbidden arts, and birthed the Nephilim — then the world changed. But this is the story of the Second Humanity, not the First.

Redemptive Insight

The purity of the First Humanity shows that Yahuah always begins His redemptive plan with a pure foundation before confronting corruption.

The First Humanity was not simply uncorrupted — they were Yahuah's blueprint for redeemed humanity. Their purity reveals what Yahusha came to restore. Their direct fellowship with Yahuah mirrors the relationship restored in the Kingdom. Their spiritual genetics preserved the Messianic lineage. Their era reveals Yahuah's pattern: Purity → Instruction → Testing → Corruption → Separation → Preservation → Redemption.

Chapter 10

The Prophetic Purpose Of The First Humanity

10.1 THE FIRST HUMANITY AS YAHUAH'S ORIGINAL BLUEPRINT FOR REDEMPTION

Not only a model of creation — but a model of salvation

Before corruption ever entered the world, Yahuah did something extraordinary: He embedded the plan of redemption into the first ten generations. This means redemption was not "reactive." Redemption did not start with sin. Redemption did not begin because Adam fell. Redemption existed before the fall. The First Humanity is not simply "the people before corruption." They are the living, historical blueprint of what Yahusha would restore, what the Kingdom will resemble, what humanity looks like under perfect fellowship, and what creation looks like before evil intervenes.

Redemptive Insight

Yahuah preserved the First Humanity so that the end of the story (Yahusha restoring all things) is anchored to the beginning of the story (the original blueprint).

10.2 THE FIRST HUMANITY AS THE FOUNDATION OF THE MESSIANIC LINE

Adam to Noah — the root of the chosen family tree

The first ten patriarchs were more than righteous men. They were the structural pillars of the lineage through which the covenant, the promises, the prophecies, and ultimately Yahusha would come. Every man carried a piece of the redemptive framework: Adam — the carrier of the proto-evangelion (first prophecy of Messiah). Seth — the restored seed. Enosh — the revealer of divine worship. Kenan — the protector of ancient knowledge. Mahalalel — the prophetic voice of praise. Yared — the one whose days mark heavenly intervention. Chanok — the prophet of the ages and the judge of the Watchers. Methushelach — the symbol of mercy delaying judgment. Lamech — the revealer of Noah's redemptive role. Noah — the carrier of purity and the covenant of survival. This is not genealogy. This is architecture. This is design. This is the skeleton of salvation history.

Redemptive Insight

Each patriarch's name, life, and actions formed a prophetic timeline leading to Yahusha — long before corruption ever began.

10.3 PROPHETIC SHADOWS OF YAHUSHA IN THE FIRST HUMANITY

The Gospel was encoded before sin multiplied

Yahuah placed prophetic shadows of Yahusha in the lives of the first patriarchs. Adam — the first "son of Elohiym" prefigures the Last Adam. Seth — "appointed seed" echoes the promised Seed of the woman. Enosh — worship and calling upon Yahuah, mirrored in Yahusha's ministry. Chanok — translation to Paradise mirrors Yahusha's victory over death. Noah — salvation through water foreshadows salvation through blood. This means Yahusha was not the solution to corruption — He was the fulfillment of the original design shown in the First Humanity.

Redemptive Insight

Redemption is not the repair of a broken world — it is the restoration of a blueprint pre-written in the first patriarchs.

10.4 THE FIRST HUMANITY AS THE DIVINE RESET TEMPLATE

When the Flood came, Yahuah did not "start over." He re-aligned the world with the original blueprint. Noah is not a new beginning — he is a continuation of the First Humanity. The Flood was never destruction for destruction's sake. It was purification, preservation, alignment, and protection of the Messianic seed. Yahuah cleansed the world to ensure the blueprint would continue until Yahusha arrived.

Redemptive Insight

The Flood shows Yahuah's commitment to restoring humanity to the purity and fellowship of the First Humanity — not abandoning it.

10.5 THE FIRST HUMANITY AS THE STANDARD THAT JUDGES ALL GENERATIONS

The First Humanity lived in purity, heard Yahuah's voice, walked with Him, preserved holiness, and maintained righteousness. This makes them the benchmark. Every later generation is measured by the original pattern, not by the corrupted world. This means the Second Humanity (post-Watchers) is judged by the First Humanity, the Third Humanity (post-resurrection) is restored to resemble the First Humanity, the Kingdom Age is patterned after the First Humanity, and Yahusha brings us back to what was lost.

Redemptive Insight

The First Humanity is the mirror Yahusha uses to show what redeemed humanity will look like in the age to come.

10.6 THE FIRST HUMANITY AS THE GUARANTOR OF THE FUTURE KINGDOM

Everything Yahusha will restore in the Kingdom Age existed first in Adam → Noah: fellowship, purity, health, spiritual clarity, long life, peace, unity, divine instruction. The First Humanity is the prototype of the Millennial Kingdom. The plan of redemption is not simply forgiveness of sins — it is the restoration of the world of Adam, Seth, Enosh, and Noah.

Redemptive Insight

The end looks like the beginning. Yahusha restores humanity to its original state, not an improvised version.

10.7 THE FIRST HUMANITY WAS THE ROOT OF THE MESSIANIC TREE

From Adam to Noah, the Messianic line was guarded, protected, preserved, sustained, and prophetically shaped. No patriarch lived by accident. Each one carried a piece of the covenant until the Redeemer would come. This line survived the fall, survived the rise of corruption, survived the Flood, and continued through Shem, Abraham, Isaac, Jacob, David... until it reached Yahusha.

Redemptive Insight

Without the First Humanity, there would be no Messiah. Their preserved purity was the womb of redemption.

The First Humanity is the blueprint, not just the beginning. Their existence reveals what Yahusha came to restore, not merely what was lost. Each patriarch carried a prophetic piece of the redemption puzzle. Their lives encoded the Gospel before corruption spread. The Flood preserved the blueprint, not reset it. The Messianic line flows directly from their preserved purity. The end-time restoration mirrors the First Humanity.

Chapter 11

The Hidden Preparation For The Coming Conflict

How Yahuah Used Time, Memory, and Mercy to Position the First Humanity

Book Two has shown us who the First Humanity was: pure, instructed, Spirit-bearing, living in a world still echoing Eden. But there is a quieter story running underneath all of that — a story rarely told: how Yahuah used time itself as a tool of mercy, how He built a collective memory strong enough to withstand future darkness, how heaven watched and recorded the first ages, and how the world was quietly positioned for the greatest conflict in human history. Book Two is not only about what the First Humanity was. It is about how Yahuah prepared them for the moment when everything would change.

11.1 TIME AS THE FIRST INSTRUMENT OF MERCY

The long lifespans before the Flood were not a random biological curiosity. They were a deliberate part of Yahuah's strategy. When Adam lived for centuries, it meant much more than personal longevity. Generation after generation could hear the story of creation from the very lips of the man who stood in the Garden. The promises, warnings, and commands of Yahuah did not pass through hundreds of anonymous intermediaries. They passed through very few mouths, repeatedly, over many centuries. The same voices that heard Yahuah personally were still speaking while new generations were born. In other words, Yahuah stretched the lives of the first patriarchs so that truth would not fragment while the world was still spiritually young.

The long ages of Adam and his descendants were a shield against distortion, a living confirmation of the beginning, and a continuous reminder that creation had a purpose and a Creator. Before battles, Yahuah secured memory. He ensured that when corruption finally came, it would not arrive in a world ignorant of truth, but in a world that had heard the truth often and clearly.

11.2 THE FORMATION OF A COVENANT MEMORY

The First Humanity was not only pure — it was being trained. Over centuries, Yahuah was not simply watching human behavior; He was shaping human identity. Through repeated instruction, shared worship, altars, offerings, prophetic words, and the testimonies of the patriarchs, a covenant memory was formed.

This memory did not consist only of doctrines, but of stories of Yahuah's goodness, recollections of Eden, testimonies of His voice, warnings about disobedience, the promise of the coming Seed, and the understanding that history itself was going somewhere.

The First Humanity did not possess scrolls as later generations would. Their Scripture was living: living men who had walked with Yahuah, living traditions guarded by fathers and elders, living worship that embedded truth into daily life. This was not nostalgia. It was preparation.

Yahuah was building something deeper than a people who behaved well. He was building a people who remembered — so that when the test came, the righteous would have something firm to hold onto.

11.3 THE SILENT WATCH OF HEAVEN

While the First Humanity walked the earth in purity, the heavens were not indifferent. Ministering spirits, righteous Watchers, and the heavenly court observed, recorded, and bore witness to the unfolding of human history.

Before the rebellion of any angel, there was a long era of

observation. The choices of men were seen, the growth of worship was noted, the responses to Yahuah's voice were weighed, and the early altars and sacrifices were remembered in heaven.

Nothing was casual. The First Humanity lived in a world without spiritual enemies, but not without spiritual attention. Their faithfulness, their failures, their worship, their obedience — all of it was writing a testimony that would later be used to judge rebellion, to justify mercy, and to demonstrate that humanity was capable of walking with Yahuah before corruption ever touched the earth.

Before any accusation could be raised, heaven already had proof: humanity, in its original state, could walk in righteousness. This silent watch of heaven is part of the preparation. When darkness later claims the world, it will not be able to say that men were made for corruption.

11.4 THE FIRST TENSIONS INSIDE THE HUMAN STORY

Though the First Humanity remained pure in nature, it was not exempt from inner tension. Over centuries, subtle dynamics appeared: the weight of distance from Eden, the pain of death entering the story, the questions that arise in a world where disobedience has consequences, and the emotional impact of loss, toil, and delay.

These were not signs of corruption. They were the first signs of human maturity: learning to trust Yahuah outside the Garden, learning to obey without seeing everything, learning to live by promise and not by sight.

In these inner tensions, reverence grew deeper, dependence became more conscious, worship gained more meaning. Yahuah was not merely preserving a pure people; He was maturing them. They were no longer just innocent — they were becoming responsible.

This inner journey would later make all the difference when the world split into two humanities. Those who clung to Yahuah did so not merely out of habit, but out of a tested relationship.

11.5 WHY THE AGE OF THE FIRST HUMANITY COULD NOT LAST FOREVER

The First Humanity was pure, preserved, and beloved. Yet its era was never meant to be the final state of creation. If the story had ended there, there would be no revelation of Yahuah's justice against corruption, no manifestation of His mercy in the midst of wickedness, no unveiling of His power to restore what had been attacked, and no revelation of Yahusha as Redeemer, Judge, and King.

The First Humanity is the foundation, not the conclusion. Yahuah allowed its era to run long enough to establish the blueprint, build the covenant memory, anchor the Messianic line, and demonstrate that His design was good. But for the fullness of His purpose to be revealed, the world would have to face opposition, distortion, and open rebellion. Not because Yahuah desired evil, but because He intended to reveal a salvation so complete that nothing — not even the worst corruption — would be able to stand against it.

The end of the First Humanity's age is not a failure of the blueprint. It is the moment when the blueprint is carried into a contested world so that redemption can be seen in its fullness.

11.6 STANDING ON THE EDGE OF TWO WORLDS

By the close of the age described in this book, the earth stands at a threshold: behind it, centuries of purity, unity, direct instruction, and covenant memory; before it, a coming collision between heaven and earth, between obedience and rebellion, between what Yahuah created and what rebellious beings will try to remake.

The First Humanity has received the breath of Elohiym, learned His ways, preserved His Name, guarded His lineage, and been trained in trust outside Eden. They are ready — not for destruction, but for testing. The next stage of the story will not begin in ignorance, but in full light.

Book Two ends with humanity still pure in nature, still carrying the Ruach, still walking under the memory of Eden, still anchored in the words of Adam, Chanok, and the patriarchs. But the horizon is darkening. A different kind of humanity is about to appear — one born not from the breath of Yahuah, but from the union of rebellious angels and mortal women.

A world that has only known uncontested light is about to face organized darkness.

11.7 WHEN HUMANITY BREAKS

Book Three will not retell the purity of the First Humanity. It will reveal how the Second Humanity emerges, how the inner tensions and external temptations finally collide, how the Watchers' rebellion tears into the human story, how the nature of mankind is challenged, altered, and weaponized, and how Yahuah's redemption plan responds to this new, brutal reality.

If Book One revealed the Works of Creation, and Book Two revealed the First Humanity in its holy beginning, then Book Three will uncover: The Fallen Nature — How the Second Humanity Was Born, and How Yahuah Refused to Abandon His Design.

The story now moves from untested purity to assaulted identity, from uncontested order to spiritual war, from quiet preparation to open conflict.

The First Humanity has been prepared. The stage is set. Heaven has watched. The testimony is written.

Now the question will be tested in the world of the Second Humanity:

What happens when a pure creation meets a corruption it was

never designed to host?

Book Two ends here — with the First Humanity standing in the light of Yahuah, on the very edge of a darkness that will try — and fail — to erase everything Yahuah has begun.

BOOK 3
THE THREE HUMANITIES

The Corruption of the Second Humanity and the Acceleration of Yahuah's Salvation Plan

THE SECOND HUMANITY

The Hybrid Line Born Without the Ruach of Elohiym

How the Watchers' Fall Produced a People Outside Redemption—and How Yahuah Preserved His Plan

Introduction

The Rise Of A Second Humanity

In the beginning, Yahuah Elohiym formed one single humanity—a pure, unified people, created through His Ruach and designed to walk in perpetual communion with Him. For nearly twelve centuries, the world remained untouched by the darkness that would one day descend from heaven. There was no corruption, no demonic influence, no genetic interference, no hybrid beings—only the natural consequences of Adam and Chawwâh's disobedience, but not yet the contamination that would emerge from the rebellion of celestial beings.

Around the fifth century of human history, Yahuah sent His holy Watchers, messengers of righteousness, to instruct mankind in the ways of life and divine order. Through them, humanity learned:

- the laws and commandments of Yahuah
- justice, righteousness, and truth
- agriculture and the cultivation of the earth
- proper conduct and relationships
- heavenly knowledge and wisdom

For generations, humanity flourished under their guidance. The world reflected the harmony Yahuah intended—a society guided by purity, righteousness, and the direct influence of the Ruach.

But around the 1,200th year, a catastrophe erupted—one that would forever divide humanity into two distinct groups.

The very Watchers who had been entrusted with teaching righteousness fell into rebellion. What began as admiration turned into lust. What began as service turned into disobedience. They abandoned their heavenly estate, took human women as wives, and forged a union forbidden in heaven and unknown on earth.

From this transgression came the beings called Nephilim—a hybrid race of giants, born with corrupted flesh, immense strength, altered DNA, and without the Ruach of Elohiym.

At that moment, humanity ceased to be one people.

Two groups now existed:

1. The Original Human Line — Pure and Ruach-Breathed

- created through the breath of Elohiym
- able to seek Yahuah
- able to repent
- able to obey
- able to carry His covenant

2. The Second Humanity — The Hybrid Line

- born without the Ruach
- unable to connect to Yahuah
- unable to repent
- predisposed entirely toward evil
- corrupting the earth simply by existing

This second group was not part of Yahuah's design.

They were not created by His will.

They did not descend from Adam through the neshama of Elohiym.

They possessed no divine spark, no spiritual consciousness, and no capacity for redemption.

Humanity had now been divided—and the world would never be the same again.

Chapter 1

The Nature Of The Second Humanity

Born Without the Ruach, Destined for Corruption

1.1 – THE BIRTH OF A HUMANITY OUTSIDE YAHUAH'S DESIGN

When the Watchers descended out of their appointed order and united themselves with the daughters of men, the result was a new kind of humanity—one that did not belong to the original creation of Yahuah. The offspring of these forbidden unions, known in Scripture as Nephilim, were extraordinary in physical strength but catastrophic in spiritual nature.

They were alive in flesh but dead in spirit. They walked the earth with immense vigor, yet lacked the divine spark that makes a human capable of knowing, loving, or obeying Yahuah.

For the first time since creation, a humanity existed that Yahuah did not form, shape, or breathe into.

This event did not merely disrupt humanity—it threatened the entire plan of salvation itself. If corruption prevailed, the line that would bring forth redemption could be erased.

1.2 – THE FUNDAMENTAL DIFFERENCE BETWEEN THE TWO HUMANITIES

Adam and Chawwâh were created with the Neshamah—the divine breath of life (Bereshith 2:7). This breath infused them with the Ruach, the divine image, the ability to commune with Yahuah, the moral capacity to obey or disobey, and the covenant identity given to humanity.

But the second humanity—the hybrid offspring of the Watchers—received none of this. Their bodies were strong, but their spirits were empty. Their minds were sharp, but their nature was estranged from Elohiym. Their existence was powerful, but entirely outside the covenant.

This division is not just biological; it is spiritual, theological, and prophetic — and it sets the stage for why Yahuah would later act to preserve the line of redemption.

1.3 – A HUMANITY ENTIRELY CARNAL AND NOT SPIRITUAL

Scripture and Enoch together explain the condition of the hybrid line: beings born without the Ruach are entirely carnal and incapable of knowing Elohiym.

1. — Enoch Reveals the Origin of a Flesh-Only Line

Chănôk (Enoch) records Yahuah's rebuke to the fallen Watchers:

> *"You were qadosh, spiritual, living the eternal life; yet you defiled yourselves with the blood of women, and have begotten children with the blood of flesh." — Enoch 15:4*

This verse exposes the spiritual crisis. The Watchers were spiritual beings. Women were flesh. Their offspring were born entirely of flesh, without the breath or Ruach of Elohiym.

This explains why the second humanity was spiritually dead from birth.

2. — "Born of flesh" means "flesh only"

Yahusha confirmed this principle:

> "That which is born of the flesh is flesh; and that which is born of the Spirit is spirit." — Yoḥanan 3:6

The second humanity was born of flesh only and therefore remained only flesh — never spirit.

3. — Enoch Confirms Their Spiritual Emptiness

Enoch goes further:

> "The spirits born from flesh and blood shall be called evil spirits on earth... because they were born from men and from the holy Watchers is their origin." — Enoch 15:8–9

This establishes that they possessed no divine breath, no spiritual life, no eternal identity, no covenant connection, and no Ruach.

They were not created to be redeemed — but Yahuah's plan of salvation included preventing this corruption from overtaking the whole earth.

4. — Paul: The Natural Man Cannot Receive the Things of Elohiym

Sha'ul confirms the condition of any being without the Ruach:

> "The natural man does not receive the things of the Spirit of Elohiym... he cannot understand them, because they are spiritually discerned." — 1 Corinthians 2:14

The Nephilim were the ultimate "natural men" — fully flesh, spiritually blind.

5. — Jude: Devoid of the Spirit

Yahudah describes beings who do not possess the Ruach:

> "These are worldly, natural, devoid of the Spirit." — Yahudah (Jude) 1:19

This fits the second humanity precisely: a people of flesh without Spirit.

1.4 – A HUMANITY WITH NO RUACH

The Nephilim and their descendants were marked by complete spiritual severance. They possessed no Ruach, no covenant capacity, no access to Yahuah, no spiritual inheritance, no ability to repent, and no redemption.

This is not merely a moral category. It is a spiritual impossibility.

The Watchers had no Ruach, so they could not transmit Ruach. Their offspring were biologically alive but spiritually empty.

This is why their presence threatened the line of salvation — and why Yahuah would soon intervene to protect the world He created and the humanity He intended to redeem.

1.5 – THE INHERITANCE OF BROKENNESS

As Enoch and Jude reveal, the Watchers lost their estate:

> *"The angels who did not keep their first estate He has reserved in everlasting chains."* — Yahudah (Jude) 1:6

Their children inherited the consequences of their rebellion. They were born already separated. Born already corrupted. Born already outside the covenant. Born already contrary to the plan of salvation.

Yet even in this darkness, Yahuah's plan did not fail. The existence of the second humanity did not cancel redemption — it revealed the necessity of it. It proved that humanity could not save itself. It showed the danger of spiritual rebellion.

It prepared the stage for the preservation of Noah, the covenant of Abraham, the line of Yasharal, and ultimately the coming of

Yahusha, the One who restores what corruption attempted to destroy.

The rise of the second humanity only magnifies the brilliance of Yahuah's salvation.

Chapter 2

The Inheritance Of The Second Humanity

The Hybrid Line Formed Without the Ruach of Yahuah

2.1 – THE DUAL INHERITANCE OF THE NEPHILIM

The Nephilim inherited traits from two different orders of creation, yet lacked the most essential one: the Ruach of Yahuah.

1. — What They Inherited from Their Angelic Fathers

From the fallen Watchers they received unnatural strength, supernatural knowledge not meant for mankind, dominion instincts and territorial aggression, a warrior temperament, spiritual rebellion, and pride and self-exaltation. These characteristics reflected the corrupted nature of their fathers — beings who were once qadosh but fell from their estate through disobedience.

2. — What They Inherited from Their Human Mothers

From mortal women they inherited mortal flesh, corruptible nature, human appetites, emotional volatility, and earthly desires. This created a hybrid condition: fleshly mortality fused with fallen heavenly traits — a mixture that Yahuah never designed.

3. — The Resulting Nature of the Second Humanity

This combination produced beings who were intellectually brilliant, physically terrifying, spiritually blind, morally corrupt, and violently dominant. They were overgrown bodies with underdeveloped souls — creatures of instinct, not covenant.

2.2 – THE ONE INHERITANCE THEY LACKED: THE RUACH OF YAHUAH

The most critical theological truth is this:

1. — Angels Cannot Transmit the Breath of Elohiym

Only Yahuah Himself can give neshamah (the breath of life) and Ruach (the spiritual capacity to know Him). The Watchers, though powerful, do not possess the Ruach — therefore they cannot transmit what they do not have.

2. — What the Hybrids Could Not Receive

Because they lacked the Ruach, the hybrid line was incapable of receiving covenant, Torah, repentance, redemption, spiritual communion, or the knowledge of Yahuah. They were like living tombs — shells of flesh with no capacity for spiritual life.

3. — Why Yahuah Did Not Call Them to Repentance

This explains three critical realities. Yahuah did not call them to repentance because repentance requires Ruach. Noach was sent to warn humans, not Nephilim, because only humans could respond. The destruction of the hybrids was not judgment — it was preservation, because their existence threatened the survival of Adam's line through which salvation would come.

2.3 – SCRIPTURE'S DESCRIPTION OF THEIR NATURE

1. — The Earthly Perspective (Bereshith 6:4)

"Mighty men... gibborim... men of renown." — Bereshith 6:4

Humans described them by their physical strength and public reputation.

2. — Heaven's Perspective (Enoch & Jubilees)

Heaven, however, describes them as abominations, corruptions, pollutions of creation, enemies of divine order, intruders into the human story, beings incompatible with covenant, and violent destroyers of the earth. Jubilees and Enoch call them spirits of wickedness, bastards of the Watchers, giants, tyrants, and devourers of mankind.

They were creatures that should never have existed, produced only because the Watchers crossed a boundary that Yahuah had eternally forbidden.

2.4 – THE ULTIMATE THEOLOGICAL ISSUE

The second humanity was not part of the creation Yahuah declared "very good."

1. — Adam's Line Was Formed Through Yahuah's Design

Adam's lineage came from divine breath, divine intention, divine purpose, divine compassion, and covenantal design.

2. — The Hybrid Line Was Formed Through Rebellion

The hybrid line originated from rebellion, lust, disobedience, spiritual transgression, and unauthorized union.

3. — They Were Not a Branch of Adam — They Were an Interruption

The second humanity was a contamination, a corruption, a foreign seed, a threat to the original creation, and an interruption to the line through which salvation would come. If allowed to spread unchecked, they could erase the very lineage through which Yahusha would later be born. Thus, the issue was not merely historical — it was redemptive, tied to the survival of Yahuah's salvation plan.

2.5 – CONCLUSION OF SECTION 1

The second humanity — born from the Watchers and mortal women — entered the world without the Ruach that makes humanity capable of knowing Elohiym. They were physically living, spiritually dead, mentally brilliant, morally bankrupt, powerful in body, and powerless in spirit.

Without the Ruach, they could not worship, repent, obey, love, receive instruction, walk in covenant, or be redeemed. They were, in essence, human bodies without the divine breath that makes a soul capable of knowing Yahuah.

This is the foundation upon which the rest of Part 2 builds — revealing how Yahuah preserved His plan of salvation in the midst of a world threatened by a corrupted race that He never created and never breathed into.

Chapter 3

Why The Second Humanity Has No Redemption

The Theological Reality of a Hybrid Existence

3.1 – BORN WITHOUT RUACH, THEREFORE BORN OUTSIDE REDEMPTION

The second group of humanity—the hybrid offspring of the Watchers and human women—did not lose the Ruach of Yahuah. They never possessed it. They were not corrupted humans. They were a different kind of being entirely—born with biological life, but without the inner spiritual capacity that connects mankind to Elohiym.

1. — They Did Not Fall: They Were Born Fallen

Adam and Chawwâh fell through disobedience. The Watchers fell through rebellion. But the hybrid offspring entered the world already in spiritual death because angels do not possess the Ruach of procreation and angels cannot transmit the divine breath Yahuah breathed into Adam. Thus, the Nephilim were not another tribe of humanity; they were a different spiritual category, born outside the covenant design.

3.2 – CONCEIVED THROUGH TRANSGRESSION, NOT CREATION. THEY DID NOT REBEL: THEY WERE BORN FROM REBELLION

Their very conception was a violation: "The sons of Elohiym... took for themselves wives from among the daughters of men." — Bereshith 6:2. Their existence began as a breach in divine order, a disruption of creation, and a fracture in the Adamic line. From their first breath, they embodied the rebellion of their fathers.

3.3 – INCAPABLE OF SEEKING YAHUAH

To seek Yahuah, a being must possess Ruach capable of repentance, a soul designed for covenant, an identity rooted in Adam's breath, the ability to submit to divine law, and spiritual inheritance. The Nephilim possessed none of these.

1. — Why They Could Not Repent

Because they did not descend from Adam's Ruach, they lacked the internal capacity for conviction, repentance, remorse, transformation, obedience, worship, and relationship. They were alive in flesh but dead in spirit. This is not moral failure. This is ontological incapacity.

3.4 – WHY YAHUAH NEVER OFFERED THEM REDEMPTION

Nowhere in Scripture does Yahuah call them to repentance, include them in covenant, send prophets to them, or offer forgiveness. Instead, they are excluded at birth, they are outside covenant lineage, their spirits become demons upon death (Jubilees + Enoch), and their bodies are destroyed in the Flood. Yahuah never commanded Noach to preach to them. Noach preached to humans capable of repentance—not to hybrid beings with no spiritual vessel. A being without Ruach cannot repent. A being without covenant identity cannot be redeemed. A being not descended from Adam's breath cannot enter Yahuah's plan of salvation.

3.5 – WHY REDEMPTION IS THEOLOGICALLY IMPOSSIBLE FOR THE HYBRIDS

Redemption requires the Ruach of Yahuah, a soul born under Adam's covenant structure, participation in the bloodline designed by Elohiym, the ability to respond to conviction, and the capacity to choose righteousness. The Nephilim have no Ruach, no covenant lineage, no inner capacity for holiness, no spiritual inheritance, and no created link to Yahuah. They were not a fallen line to be restored. They were an intrusive line that threatened the existence of the one line through which salvation would come.

3.6 – AND YET... THE PLAN OF SALVATION SURVIVED

While the hybrid race filled the earth with violence and terror (Bereshith 6:11–12), Yahuah preserved a single family: Noach — "Perfect in His Generations," meaning perfect in lineage, uncorrupted in bloodline. Through Noach, Yahuah ensured the preservation of Adam's Ruach, the continuation of the true human line, the seed through which Messiah would come, the maintenance of spiritual inheritance, and the possibility of redemption for creation. Even as hybrid corruption threatened the earth, redemption was carried inside the ark—protected, preserved, and destined for fulfillment.

3.7 – SUMMARY THOUGHT

The second humanity had no redemption not because Yahuah lacked mercy, but because they lacked the essence that makes mercy receivable. And yet the mercy of Yahuah shines brilliantly: He preserved the pure line of Adam—the only line capable of receiving salvation, carrying covenant, and ultimately bringing forth Yahusha.

Chapter 4

The Mercy Of Yahuah Amid Rising Corruption

Noach: The Final Pure Seed and the Bridge of Redemption

4.1 – A MIRACULOUS BIRTH IN A DYING WORLD

As the second humanity multiplied across the earth—hybrid, lawless, and spiritually dead—something unprecedented occurred within the remaining pure line of Adam. In the days of Lamech, a child was born whose very appearance terrified his father, with skin shining like snow, hair white like wool, eyes glowing like the sun, and a mouth that spoke heavenly wisdom from birth. This child was Noach — the final seed of purity, the last man born with an unbroken Ruach inheritance from Adam.

> 1. — Jubilees Records the Mystery
>
> Jubilees declares that Noach's birth was unlike any before him, a miraculous act of preservation by Yahuah to ensure that the covenant, the promise, and ultimately salvation would not perish from the earth.

4.2 – NOACH: THE PRESERVED SEED OF ADAM

> 1. — The Last Man Untouched by Hybrid Corruption

As hybrid corruption spread through the daughters of men, the pure line of Adam was slowly disappearing. Had Yahuah not intervened, the covenant line would have been extinguished — and with it the possibility of redemption for all future generations. But in His mercy, Yahuah raised Noach as the final uncorrupted descendant of Adam, the carrier of the original Ruach-breath, the vessel through whom humanity would survive, and the one man whose righteousness stood in contrast to an entire world collapsing into violence.

2. — "Perfect in His Generations" — Bereshith 6:9

"Noach was a righteous man, perfect in his generations." "tâmîym dôr" means his lineage was uncorrupted, his ancestry undefiled, and his bloodline untouched by angelic genetic pollution. Noach was the last safeguard of the creation Yahuah had originally made — the final living connection to Adam's breath and identity.

4.3 – RAISED BY YAHUAH FROM BIRTH

According to Jubilees, Noach spoke with Yahuah from the moment his was born, was visited and instructed by the Angels of the Presence, learned the heavenly laws written on the tablets of Heaven, and grew in wisdom and holiness before Yahuah.

1. — The Contrast Between Two Lines

While the second humanity grew mighty in violence, Noach grew mighty in righteousness. While hybrid tyrants spread terror, Noach spread obedience. While Nephilim darkened the earth, Noach carried the last lamp of divine truth. He embodied the reality that even when the world descends into corruption, Yahuah sustains one righteous line.

4.4 – NOACH: A SIGN OF MERCY BEFORE JUDGMENT

Noach's birth was not only miraculous — it was prophetic. In the midst of genetic corruption, spiritual ruin, hybrid tyranny, the pollution of creation, and the collapse of human purity, Yahuah revealed His mercy.

1. — Noach Is the Bridge of Salvation

Noach connects the first creation to the renewed earth, pure humanity to surviving humanity, Adam's lineage to the covenant line, and the world before the Flood to the world after. Noach is the proof that Yahuah's plan of salvation does not depend on human faithfulness — but on Yahuah's mercy, foresight, and unbreakable promises.

4.5 – WHEN DARKNESS RISES, MERCY RISES HIGHER

As the hybrid race spread, as violence overwhelmed the earth, as the Nephilim devoured creation, and as humanity plunged into ruin — Yahuah did not abandon the world. He raised a man from the womb, prepared him from infancy, preserved him in purity, and appointed him for the salvation of the chosen seed.

1. — The Heart of the Redemption Narrative

Even when humanity destroys what Yahuah created, Yahuah creates a new way forward. The birth of Noach is not simply history — it is a declaration: the mercy of Yahuah rises before His judgment. The plan of salvation begins before the Flood waters fall. No darkness is strong enough to extinguish the seed Yahuah chooses to preserve.

4.6 – SUMMARY THOUGHT

The rise of the second humanity brought corruption, violence, and near extinction to Adam's line. But the birth of Noach proves that the mercy of Yahuah is stronger than the corruption of the Watchers. Noach stands as the preserved line, the final pure seed, the bridge of redemption, the testimony that salvation is rooted in Yahuah's mercy, and the assurance that His plan cannot be destroyed by rebellion. Even at the darkest moment of human history, the plan of salvation was already alive — inside the womb of a child named Noach.

Chapter 5

The Two-Part Redemptive Plan Of Yahuah
Why the Flood Was Salvation — Not Destruction

5.1 – UNDERSTANDING THE FLOOD THROUGH THE LENS OF REDEMPTION

When the second humanity—the hybrid offspring of the Watchers—spread across the earth, Yahuah did not respond with impulsive wrath or arbitrary destruction. Scripture and the ancient writings reveal the opposite truth: the Flood was mercy, not annihilation, a rescue mission, not a vendetta, the preservation of salvation's future, not the end of creation.

To save humanity, Yahuah executed a two-part redemptive plan:

Preserve the covenant lineage.

Purge the corruption that threatened to erase it.

PART 1 – PRESERVE THE PURE SEED

5.2 – SALVATION PREPARED BEFORE JUDGMENT

Before judgment ever fell, Yahuah had already secured a path for salvation. He preserved every essential element necessary for the continuation of the uncorrupted creation. Noach was tâmîym dôr, perfect in his generations. Noach's wife was likewise pure in lineage. Shem, Ham, and Yapheth carried uncorrupted human seed. Their wives were preserved from hybrid contamination.

Seven pairs of all clean animals and one pair of every unclean animal were prepared. The covenant from Adam to Seth to Enosh to Enoch to Noach was preserved. The heavenly laws and knowledge were protected through Noach. The entire foundation of humanity and creation was secured.

This was not random. This was intentional preservation by divine wisdom.

1. — Why This Preservation Was Essential

Through Noach, Yahuah safeguarded the continuation of life, the purity of the Adamic line, the covenant of creation, the prophetic lineage that leads to Messiah, the possibility of human salvation, and the integrity of spiritual inheritance.

If Noach perished, redemption could not enter the world. The Messiah could not be born. Humanity could not be saved.

PART 2 – PURGE THE CORRUPTED SEED

5.3 – WHY THE FLOOD WAS NECESSARY TO SAVE CREATION

The world before the Flood was not merely sinful. It had become biologically, genetically, spiritually, and morally corrupted by hybrid entities never intended to exist.

Here is the full picture.

5.4 – THE EARTH WAS FILLED WITH VIOLENCE (BERESHITH 6:11)

The hybrids—the Nephilim and their sub-breeds—did not merely commit sin. They destroyed the created order.

Enoch describes their violence: "And they began to sin against birds, beasts, reptiles, and fish..."

The ancient records show that Nephilim killed Nephiyl, Nephiyl killed Eliyo, Eliyo killed the second-group humans, and the corrupted second-group humans slaughtered one another.

This was not human wickedness. This was creation collapsing.

The hybrids were giants, cannibals, predators of animals and humans, mentally unstable, spiritually dead, and obsessed with domination and bloodshed. They were literal forces of destruction.

5.5 – THEY DEVOURED THE EARTH'S RESOURCES (ENOCH 7:4-6; JUBILEES 7:22)

The giants consumed all human labor, stripped the land of food, ate animals alive, drank blood, and eventually began eating humans. "And they began to devour mankind... and drink the blood..."

When food ran out, they devoured each other.

Creation was becoming unsustainable.

If Yahuah had not intervened, humanity would vanish, animals would disappear, the earth would collapse, and hybrid DNA would dominate all life.

This was not moral decline — it was a total corruption of all flesh.

5.6 – THE WATCHERS CORRUPTED ALL CREATION (JUBILEES 5; ENOCH 8)

The fallen Watchers brought forbidden knowledge. They introduced weapons and metallurgy, enchantments and sorcery, genetic mixing, root-cutting and alchemy, warfare strategies, occult knowledge, forbidden sciences, and mixtures of species.

Enoch records that Azazel taught men to make swords and

bracelets and the beautifying of the eyelids and every kind of precious stone and dye.

Jubilees adds that the Watchers sinned against the beasts and the birds, indicating genetic tampering.

Humanity altered plants, animals, metals, medicines, and even the human body.

Creation as Yahuah designed it was being rewritten.

If Yahuah delayed even one generation, there would be nothing left to save.

5.7 – THE SECOND HUMANITY COULD NOT BE REDEEMED

Because the hybrids had no Ruach, no covenant identity, no eternal breath, no capacity for repentance, and no spiritual conscience, they were born spiritually dead.

They were not punished — they were removed, like a tumor that would have killed the entire body.

The Flood was not destruction. It was surgery.

5.8 – THE FLOOD SAVED THE WORLD FROM ETERNAL RUIN

Had the hybrids survived, no Messiah could be born, no covenant could stand, no human soul could exist, no salvation could be offered, Adam's line would be erased, and Yahuah's image would vanish from the earth.

The Flood restored the possibility of redemption. It re-established purity. It halted biological corruption. It removed the threat to salvation.

Without the Flood, light would be extinguished, truth would vanish, covenant lineage would dissolve, and humanity would cease to exist.

Thus the Flood was an act of mercy, restoration, preservation, and salvation.

5.9 – THE TWO-PART REDEMPTIVE PLAN

Yahuah's plan ensured that the covenant seed survived through Noach and his family and that the corrupted seed was removed so creation could be restored.

The Foundational Equation Behind the Flood

Angels Watchers + human women = children without the Ruach of Elohiym.

Angels, the Watchers, united with human women and produced children without the Ruach of Elohiym.

This occurred because angels do not possess the procreation gene, angels were never created to transmit life, angels cannot pass the Ruach, and only man was created with the ability to procreate children who carry the divine breath.

Only Adam's lineage can produce beings with the Ruach of Elohiym, covenant identity, spiritual capacity, and the ability to know Yahuah.

The hybrid offspring had biological life, but no Ruach, because they were never part of Yahuah's design for human reproduction.

This equation explains the entire necessity of the Flood.

Only the line that carries the Ruach could carry the plan of salvation.

3. THE TURNING POINT OF HUMAN HISTORY

The Flood was not merely judgment — it was the reset that

allowed redemption to continue.

Even though the corrupted line attempted to survive by constructing their own vessels, only one boat survived.

From this moment forward, the story of redemption moves with renewed clarity.

The pure seed was preserved.

The corrupted seed was removed.

Salvation was protected.

Covenant was secured.

The path to Messiah remained alive.

Chapter 6

After The Flood: The Giants Rise Again

The Survival, Spread, and Identification of
the Post-Flood Nephilim

6.1 – A REMNANT SURVIVES: THE SECOND HUMANITY AFTER THE FLOOD

Scripture is clear: though Yahuah purged the earth through the Flood, a remnant of the hybrid lineage survived — not through the Ark of Noach, but through a separate vessel built by the fallen lineage itself. This explains the presence of giants after the Flood in the days of Mosheh, Yahusha, Dawid, and the Prophets. To understand redemption's path moving forward, we must trace how they survived, where they landed, where they migrated, and how they appear in Scripture.

6.2 – THE NEPHILIM VESSEL SURVIVES THE FLOOD

Ancient sources — including Enoch, Jubilees, and extra-biblical records like the Book of the Nephilim (Enki traditions) — confirm that the hybrid race, knowing judgment was coming, constructed multiple vessels. All were destroyed except one. What this preserved was hybrid DNA, the corrupted lineage, the rebellious spiritual inheritance, and the continuation of the second humanity. This answers a biblical mystery: Why do giants reappear after the Flood? Because a remnant survived outside Noach's Ark.

6.3 – WHERE THE NEPHILIM LANDED: ARRAT / ARARAT

1. — Noach's Ark Landed at Mount Lubar, Mountains of Ararat

Jubilees 5:28–29 states clearly that "The ark rested on the mountains of Lubar." Lubar refers to the Armenian highlands (ancient Urartu), not modern Turkey. This region was long called The Land of Noach.

2. — The Nephilim Craft Landed Elsewhere

The hybrid vessel landed in Arrat, later called Ararat, a different ridge in ancient Turkey, mentioned in Mesopotamian records. Thus, Noach's Ark rested at Lubar in Armenia, while the Nephilim vessel landed in Arrat in Turkey. From Arrat, the hybrid survivors traveled southward.

6.4 – THE NEPHILIM DESCEND INTO SHINAR / SENAAR / BABEL – SCRIPTURE CONFIRMATION

Bereshith 11:2 states, "They journeyed from the east and settled in the land of Shinar." Jubilees 10 calls the region Senaar. Ancient Akkadian refers to it as Šinar or Šanar. This region became the first post-Flood headquarters of the hybrid race, the birthplace of Babel, the homeland of Nimrod, and the launchpad of post-Flood rebellion against Heaven. Their path was Arrat → Shinar → Babel, exactly as Scripture says.

6.5 — Babel: The First Post-Flood Hybrid Kingdom

The remnant hybrid race established their first kingdom in Senaar/Babel, where they built fortified cities, erected temples and ziggurats, recreated forbidden pre-Flood knowledge, united under rebellious leadership, and sought access to the heavens. Their intent was not architectural ambition: "Let us build a tower... whose top may reach unto the heavens" (Bereshith 11:4). This was the continuation of the Watchers' rebellion, attempting to reenter the heavenly realm by force.

6.6 – YAHUAH'S RESPONSE AT BABEL: SALVATION, NOT DESTRUCTION

Yahuah did not destroy Babel's builders. He saved humanity from them. He intervened by confusing their languages, scattering them over the earth, breaking their unity, and dismantling their kingdom. This was mercy, not wrath. Jubilees 10 records that if united, they would have corrupted the whole world again, enslaved all nations, extinguished the pure human lineage, and attempted another heavenly rebellion. Confusion of languages was salvation for mankind, preventing a second global corruption.

6.7 – THE NATIONS OF CHAM AND THE RISE OF POST-FLOOD HYBRID DOMINION

How Nimrod, Cham's Descendants, and the Hybrid Tribes Recreated the Corruption of the First World.

The Scriptures and ancient records reveal a terrifying continuity: the same corruption that destroyed the First World began rising again after the Flood through the line of Cham and especially through Nimrod. This section exposes the genealogical roots, the geopolitical rise, the spiritual rebellion, the hybrid resurgence, and the covenantal threat that shaped the entire biblical landscape of the Second Humanity. All of it converges into one truth: the post-Flood giants did not arise at random — they emerged through the same spiritual corruption revived by Nimrod.

1. — THE LINE OF CHAM: THE FIRST POST-FLOOD OPENING TO NEPHILIM INFLUENCE

Scripture is explicit: "And the sons of Châm: Kûsh, and Mitsrayim, and Pûṭ, and Kena'an" (Berēshīṯh 10:6). Cham's four sons become the founders of the most spiritually hostile nations surrounding Yasharal. Kush became Ethiopia and Nubia. Mitsrayim became Egypt. Put became Libya. Canaan became all Canaanite nations. These nations are repeatedly described as practicing sorcery, idolatry, child sacrifice, hybridization, and Nephilim-style corruption. This is not accidental. The revival of the Nephilim system begins here — in Cham's lineage.

2. — NIMROD WAS NOT A NEPHILIM, BUT HE OPENED THE DOOR

Nimrod reveals the post-Flood pattern. He was born human, yet he became Nephilim-like. He revived the first world's corruption. He birthed Babel and Assyria. His system produced Philistine hybrid warriors. Thus, Cham's line becomes the first post-Flood environment for hybrid resurgence, and Nimrod becomes the human access point for demonic re-entry.

3. — IDENTIFYING THE POST-FLOOD HYBRID LINEAGES

Now this naturally transitions into the catalog of all hybrid tribes — and with the Nimrod foundation already laid, the flow becomes perfect and chronological.

4. — NEPHIYL (לִיפָנ) — "THE FALLEN ONES"

(Original Root of All Hybrid Tribes)

Scripture: Bereshith 6:4; Bamidbar 13:33.

The Nephilim are the children of the Watchers (fallen angels) and human women. Their name means "fallen ones," born of those who fell. They are the original hybrid giants of the First Humanity and the source of all later hybrid clans.

5. — REPHA'IM (םיִאָפְר) — THE DOMINANT POST-FLOOD HYBRID POLITY

Scripture: Debariym 3; Yahusha; Shemu'el; Melakim.

History: Ugaritic "rpum" warrior spirits.

The Rephaim become the central giant confederation, including Og of Bashan, the Valley of Rephaim, and numerous warrior clans. They are the primary hybrid nations encountered by Yasharal.

6. — ANAKIM (עֲנָקִים) — "THE LONG-NECKED, THE TALL ONES"

Scripture: Bamidbar 13; Debariym 1; Yahusha 11.

The Anakim are descendants of Anak, known for towering height, immense strength, and intimidation. Their connection to the Anunnaki is reflected linguistically: ANAQ → ANAK → ANAKIM → ANAQIY → ANUNNAKI. All belong to the same lineage, which pagan cultures later deified.

7. — EMIM — "THE TERRIFYING ONES"

Scripture: Debariym 2:10–11.

A giant people in Moab, identified as Rephaim.

8. — ZAMZUMMIM — WARLIKE GIANT TRIBE

Scripture: Debariym 2:20.

Feared and mighty. Also counted among the Rephaim.

9. — ZUZIM — EARLY POST-FLOOD GIANTS

Scripture: Bereshith 14:5.

A branch of hybrid warriors encountered in the war of the kings.

10. — OG OF BASHAN — LAST GREAT KING OF THE REPHA'IM

Scripture: Debariym 3:11.

His 13-foot iron bed testifies to his size. His land, Bashan, is the core hybrid territory.

11. — GOLYATH (GOLIATH) OF GATH

Scripture: 1 Shemu'el 17; 2 Shemu'el 21.

Not a freak exception — he is part of the Philistine hybrid bloodline.

12. — THE "SONS OF THE GIANT" — FINAL HYBRID REMNANTS

Scripture: 2 Shemu'el 21.

Includes Ishbi-benob, Saph, Lahmi, and the six-fingered warrior. These represent the last concentrated hybrid opposition.

13. — ONE LINEAGE, ONE CORRUPTION, ONE THREAT

All these tribes — Nephilim, Rephaim, Anakim, Emim, Zamzummim, Zuzim, Og, Goliath, and more — are branches of the same post-Flood hybrid lineage. Different names. Different locations. Different myths. One origin. One rebellion. One purpose: to oppose the plan of salvation. This is why Yahuah scattered Babel, why Yahuah empowered Yasharal, why Yahuah eliminated hybrid strongholds, why Yahuah preserved the covenant lineage, and why Yahusha came through the pure Adamic line. Redemption history advances because Yahuah protected the world from the corrupted second race.

6.8 – WHY THIS MATTERS FOR THE PLAN OF SALVATION

Yahuah's plan of salvation is always aimed at preserving His creation from corruption. The giants were a threat to the covenant, to Adam's lineage, to the human soul, to the arrival of Messiah, to pure worship, and to the knowledge of Yahuah. This explains why Babel had to be scattered, why specific tribes were commanded to be removed, why Noach's purity mattered, why Yasharal was chosen as a covenant nation, and why Yahusha came through a preserved lineage. Every step is strategic. Every action is redemptive. Every intervention protects the Messianic promise.

6.9 – FINAL SUMMARY OF SECTION 5

The Nephilim survived the Flood through their own vessel, not the Ark of Noach. They landed in Arrat and migrated to Shinar/Babel. They built the first post-Flood hybrid kingdom. Yahuah scattered them to stop a second corruption of all flesh. Scripture identifies them clearly: Nephiyl, Repha'im, Anakim, Emim, Zuzim, Zamzummim, Og, Goliath, and more. Their presence explains the violent nations Yasharal encountered. And through all of this, Yahuah preserved the pure seed — the only line through which Yahusha would come. The survival of giants is not a side story. It is a battleground of redemption.

Chapter 7

Scripture Follows The Pure Line, Not The Hybrid One

The Narrative Principle Originated by Yahuah

7.1 – THE FOUNDATIONAL KEY TO INTERPRETING THE BIBLE

One of the greatest keys for understanding Scripture is this unshakeable truth: the Bible is not the record of all humanity. It is the record of the redeemed humanity. It follows the lineage through which the plan of salvation flows — the line chosen, protected, purified, and guided to bring forth the Mashiyach. This narrative structure is not the invention of rabbis, theologians, or historians. It is a storytelling principle that originates with Yahuah Himself.

Like every great story, there is a protagonist, a central heroic arc, a redemptive journey, characters essential to victory, and one lineage that carries the destiny forward. The Scriptures follow this pattern intentionally. Yahuah reveals only what is relevant to the covenant line, not everything that existed. This principle becomes unmistakable when we examine three clear examples.

7.2 – EXAMPLE 1: ADAM'S CHILDREN AND THE SELECTIVE GENEALOGY - SCRIPTURE HIGHLIGHTS SETH, NOT EVERY CHILD

Many assume Adam and Chawwâh had only three sons — Qayin, Hebel, and Sheth — because only these three are emphasized. But this is not a limitation of history; it is a limitation of what is necessary for the covenant storyline.

Scripture hints at a much larger population. Where did Qayin's wife come from? Where did Sheth's wife come from? How could cities form so early? Jubilees fills in the historical details. Adam and Chawwâh had many sons and daughters (Jub. 4:10). Qayin married his sister Âwân (Jub. 4:9). Sheth married his sister Azûrâ (Jub. 4:11). Adam and Chawwâh had nine additional sons beyond the three named (Jub. 4:10). Thus, Scripture focuses on Seth's line because it is the line of redemption — the line leading to Mashiach. The rest existed but had no part in the covenant story.

7.3 – EXAMPLE 2: MIRYAM AND YOSEPH'S CHILDREN AND THE MESSIANIC FOCUS – SCRIPTURE FOCUSES ON YAHUSHA, NOT EVERY SIBLING

The Renewed Covenant writings follow the same divine principle. The Gospels do not list all of Miryam and Yoseph's children — not because they didn't exist, but because they are not central to the Messianic mission.

Yet Scripture clearly confirms Yahusha had siblings. "His brethren: Yaăqôb, Yôsêph, Shimôn, Yahûdâh" (Matt. 13:55). "His sisters, are they not all with us?" (Matt. 13:56). His mother and brothers sought Him (Luke 8:19). Sha'ul mentions "Yaăqôb, the brother of Âdônây" (Gal. 1:19). His brothers are listed among the disciples (Acts 1:14). The Bible is consistent: it highlights only what is essential to the divine mission. The emphasis is not on the household of Miryam but on the calling of Yahusha.

7.4 – EXAMPLE 3: PETER'S WIFE AND THE SELECTIVE APOSTOLIC FOCUS – PETER HAD A WIFE – SCRIPTURE SIMPLY DIDN'T NAME HER

Kêph had a wife because Yahusha healed Peter's mother-in-law (Matt. 8:14–15), and Sha'ul affirms Peter traveled with his wife (1 Cor. 9:5). Why is she never named? Not because she didn't exist, but because her name contributes nothing to the covenant storyline. Again: what Scripture does not name is not nonexistent — it is simply not necessary for redemption.

7.5 – THE SCRIPTURES FOLLOW ONE LINE: THE LINE OF REDEMPTION

This is the genealogical river Scripture follows: Sheth, Enosh, Kenan, Mahalalel, Yared, Enoch, Methuselah, Lamech, Noach, Shem, Eber, Abraham, Yitschaq, Ya'aqov, Yahudah, Dawid, Yahusha ha'Mashiach. This is one unbroken river — the river of redemption. Scripture follows the river, not the mud around it. All other lines, though real, are irrelevant to the covenant purpose.

7.6 – WHY SCRIPTURE DOES NOT FOLLOW THE HYBRID LINES

The descendants of the Nephilim, the Repha'im, the Emim, the Anakim, the Zamzummim, the Zuzim, and all hybrid tribes existed, thrived, and influenced history. But they did not bear the Ruach, did not carry Adam's breath, did not have the capacity for redemption, were not part of the covenant, and were not part of the promise.

They existed parallel to the covenant line but not inside it. Thus the Bible mentions them only when they collide with redemption, such as giants in the land of Kana'an, Og of Bashan, Anakim in Hebron, Emim in Moab, Zamzummim in Ammon, and Golyath of Gath. They are the antagonists, not the protagonists. The Bible is not anthropology. It is a covenant document.

7.7 – SCRIPTURE'S FOCUS REVEALS YAHUAH'S HEART

Yahuah highlights Enoch who walked with Elohiym, Noach who was perfect in his generations, Abraham the friend of Elohiym,

Yitschaq the child of promise, Ya'aqob the chosen vessel, Yahudah the royal line, Dawid the man after Yahuah's heart, and Yahusha the Redeemer of creation.

He does not focus on Nimrod's kingdom, the Anakim empires, the Emim in Moab, the Repha'im strongholds, or Philistine hybrid dynasties. This is because Yahuah reveals what advances salvation, not everything that happened in world history.

7.8 – YAHUAH IS THE ORIGINAL AUTHOR OF PROTAGONIST-FOCUSED STORYTELLING

Every human story — film, epic, novel, or myth — follows the divine blueprint: a chosen line, a heroic lineage, a mission of redemption, a conflict with darkness, a final victory. Human storytelling imitates the pattern Yahuah designed. Scripture is the original narrative structure. Yahuah selects the characters, directs the storyline, removes irrelevant branches, preserves the protagonist, and brings the Redeemer through the chosen line. All other stories echo the one Yahuah wrote.

7.9 – FINAL TRUTH

The Bible is the story of redemption, not the story of every bloodline. It follows the line of salvation, the carriers of covenant, the heirs of promise, and the pure seed that leads to Yahusha. The hybrids existed, but they were never the focus because they were never the carriers of redemption. Yahuah's Word follows the one lineage through whom He would bring forth Yahusha ha'Mashiach, the Light of the World, the Seed of the Woman, the One who crushes the nachash's head. This is why Scripture follows the pure line — because the pure line carries the plan of salvation for all creation.

Chapter 8

The Error Of Qeynan (Kenan)

The Man Who Reopened The Door Of Corruption
The Father of Post-Flood Occultism

8.1 – WHEN THE EARTH WAS CLEAN AGAIN

After the Flood, the waters receded and the ark rested. Yahuah renewed His covenant with Noach and his sons: "And I, behold, I establish My covenant with you, and with your seed after you." — Bereshith (Genesis) 9:9. For a brief moment purity reigned, violence had ceased, and the Ruach of Yahuah still rested upon the descendants of Noach. But the pattern of human history soon returned: Yahuah builds, man endangers, Yahuah redeems. Into this renewed world steps one of the most dangerous figures of the early post-Flood age: Qeynan (Kenan), a descendant of Ham, a man of relentless curiosity, a man whose curiosity would reopen a door Yahuah had closed.

8.2 – QEYNAN DISCOVERS THE INSCRIPTIONS OF THE NEPHILIM

The Book of Yôbêl (Jubilees) preserves a crucial detail that Bereshith only implies. Yôbêl 8:2–3 tells us that Qeynan "found a writing which the former generations had engraved on the rock... and he read what was thereon, and he transcribed it... and he sinned because of it, for it contained the teaching of the Watchers..." Those ancient inscriptions contained occult symbols, astrological omens, enchantments, sorcery formulas, and "the signs of heaven" taught by the Watchers. These were the very teachings that had corrupted the first world (1 Enoch 7–8). The Flood should have buried this knowledge forever, but Qeynan found it.

8.3 – QEYNAN COPIES THE FORBIDDEN KNOWLEDGE

Instead of destroying the stones, he preserved them, he transcribed them, he turned them into new tablets. Yôbêl 8:3 emphasizes that his sin was in "transcribing" the teaching of the Watchers. By copying those writings, Qeynan resurrected pre-Flood occult science, reactivated forbidden astronomy and astrology, and reintroduced the spiritual protocols of the Nephilim. He became the first post-Flood scribe of darkness.

8.4 – QEYNAN TEACHES WHAT HE COPIED

What is preserved in secret will eventually be taught in public. From that point forward, Qeynan acted as a teacher of occult arts, a guardian of forbidden knowledge, a transmitter of the Watchers' wisdom, and the first post-Flood master of sorcery. Through him, the practices that had polluted the first age now infiltrated the second. Sorcery returned, root-cutting returned, blood-magic returned, astral divination returned, spirit manipulation returned. He was not a Nephilim by blood, but he walked in the path of the Nephilim by doctrine.

8.5 – QEYNAN REOPENS A DOOR YAHUAH HAD CLOSED

The Flood had sealed the portal of corruption. Yahuah said: "The end of all flesh is come before Me; for the earth is filled with violence through them." — Bereshith 6:13. Qeynan's actions reopened the very channel of corruption Yahuah had judged. Through him, the world again began to move toward spiritual rebellion, counterfeit worship, hybrid-style thinking, and the desire to be "like the mighty ones" (gibborim).

8.6 – FROM QEYNAN'S OCCULTISM TO THE TOWER

OF BABEL

Qeynan's sin forms the theological bridge between the purified post-Flood generation and the rebellion at Babel (Bereshith 11). Once occult knowledge enters a society, it inevitably produces unity in wickedness, counterfeit spirituality, arrogant self-exaltation, and rebellion against the true Elohiym. Out of this soil will rise Nimrod, the mighty hunter before Yahuah (Bereshith 10:8–10), Babel, the first post-Flood empire of rebellion (Bereshith 11:1–4), and the Tower, a human attempt to reach the heavens by forbidden means. Qeynan is the first domino. Babel is the visible tower at the end of that line.

8.7 – THE THEOLOGICAL SIGNIFICANCE OF QEYNAN IN THE PLAN OF SALVATION

Sin enters through disobedience. Corruption enters through forbidden knowledge. Adam and Chawwâh disobeyed a direct command (Bereshith 3). The Watchers corrupted creation with revelation never meant for man (1 Enoch 7–8). Qeynan resurrected that same forbidden knowledge after the Flood (Yôbêl 8). Yet even here, Yahuah's mercy shines. While Qeynan is copying the teachings of the Watchers, Yahuah is already preparing another line: from Shem to Eber to Abram (Abraham).

This is already covenant language. Later, Yahuah calls Abram: "Get you out of your country... unto a land that I will show you... and in you shall all families of the earth be blessed." — Bereshith 12:1–3. So we have a contrast. Qeynan is the man who resurrected darkness. Abraham is the man who resurrects faith in the true Elohiym. Qeynan revived the doctrines of the Nephilim, copied the tablets of the Watchers, opened the way to Babel, and spread forbidden knowledge. Abraham restored the worship of Yahuah, received the covenant of promise, opened the way to a chosen nation, and spread obedience and faith. Qeynan is the counter-testimony of the post-Flood world, showing how quickly humanity can fall again. Abraham is the answer, showing that the plan of salvation will not be stopped.

8.8 – CLOSING OF SECTION 7

Qeynan's error is not a side note in history. It is the moment when the second age begins to mirror the first, the teachings of the Watchers return, the road to Babel is paved, and the need for a new covenant line becomes obvious. Yet even as Qeynan revives darkness, Yahuah is already moving, preserving the blessing through Shem, guarding the line of Eber, calling Abraham out of Ur, preparing the covenant, and guiding history toward Yahusha. The plan of salvation never pauses. Wherever corruption is resurrected, Yahuah raises a new standard of redemption.

Chapter 9

The Nephilim After The Flood

Babel, Shinar, And The First Post-Flood Kingdom Of Darkness
The Second Humanity Attempts to Rebuild Its Empire

9.1 – TWO VESSELS, TWO MOUNTAINS, TWO HUMANITIES

When the floodwaters receded, two vessels rested on two very different mountains. The Ark of Noach rested upon the mountains of Ararat, as Bereshith 8:4 records. This was not the modern volcanic cone of Turkey, but the ancient Lubar range in Armenia, as Yôbêl (Jubilees) 5:28–29 and 7:1 confirm. The second vessel was the vessel of the Nephilim. Extra-biblical Mesopotamian records (Atra-hasis, Enki tablets, "Book of the Nephilim") describe a hybrid vessel built by the corrupted line, designed to save the last of the giant offspring, and landing on Mount Arrat in the western Ararat region of ancient Turkey. Thus, after the Flood, the pure line began from Mount Lubar and the corrupted line began from Mount Arrat. Two mountains, two humanities, two destinies.

9.2 – THE NEPHILIM DESCEND INTO SHINAR

"And they journeyed from the east, and found a plain in the land of Shinar, and dwelt there." — Bereshith 11:2. Yôbêl 10:18 calls this region "the land of Senaar," and Yôbêl 10:25 explains that "for this reason the whole land of Shinâr is called Bâbel." This migration marks the first organized movement of the hybrid remnant. Shinar was chosen because it was fertile, irrigated by the Tigris and Euphrates, centrally located, connected to ancient pre-Flood Watcher sites, and ideal for rapid imperial expansion. It became the cradle of hybrid civilization.

9.3 – THE FIRST POST-FLOOD NEPHILIM EMPIRE: BABEL

Immediately upon settling, the hybrid clans began constructing a capital, a fortress, a technological tower, a centralized government, and a unified rebellion. "Come, let us build us a city and a tower whose head may reach into the heavens..." — Bereshith 11:4. This was not a human scientific project; it was a hybrid spiritual rebellion. They attempted to reenter the heavenly realm, revive pre-Flood dominion, centralize hybrid power under one language, one government, one tower, one rebellion, and defy Yahuah's boundaries by breaking the separation between earth and shamayim. Babel was the first anti-Yahuah empire after the Flood.

9.4 – BABEL WAS NOT A HUMAN PROJECT – IT WAS HYBRID

The builders were not primarily the descendants of Noach. They were the surviving hybrid clans: the children of the Nephilim fathers, the inheritors of corrupted DNA, the carriers of forbidden knowledge, and the offspring empowered by the spirits of the Nephilim (1 Enoch 15–16). They possessed extraordinary intellect, pre-Flood architectural secrets, astronomical knowledge, and the occult formulas Qeynan copied (Yôbêl 8:2–3). This enabled them to construct walls, structures, towers, and monuments at scales impossible for early post-Flood humanity.

9.5 – YAHUAH'S INTERVENTION AT BABEL: MERCY, NOT WRATH

If the hybrids had succeeded at Babel, they would have enslaved the whole earth, corrupted all remaining pure bloodlines, restored Watcher dominion, attempted a second heavenly invasion, and eliminated the possibility of redemption. Therefore Yahuah intervened — not to punish randomly, but to preserve salvation.

"Come, let Us go down and confound their language..." — Bereshith 11:7. Yahuah confused their languages, dismantled their unity, destroyed their technological alignment, broke their occult coordination, scattered them across the earth, halted a global hybrid empire, and preserved the line of redemption through Shem. Just as the Flood saved humanity from genetic corruption, the confusion of languages saved humanity from spiritual corruption.

9.6 – THE SCATTERING OF THE HYBRID NATIONS

Once divided linguistically, the hybrid clans dispersed into the ancient world, forming the giant nations Scripture later identifies: Repha'im, Anakim, Emim, Zamzummim, Zuzim, Avim, Amorite giant lineages, Girgashites, Philistine hybrid lines, and Nephiyl remnants. Their geographic spread included Canaan, Bashan, Mesopotamia, Anatolia, Arabia, North Africa, the Aegean, the Levant, and parts of the Mediterranean. This explains why Yasharal repeatedly encounters them in the conquest under Yahusha, in the wars of Dawid, in the days of the Judges, and in the prophetic writings. Their scattering explains the presence of giants after the Flood.

9.7 – THE SALVATION PURPOSE BEHIND THE DISPERSION

Every action Yahuah takes flows from a salvation motive. By scattering the hybrid nations, Yahuah ensured that they would never unite again, never rebuild a global anti-Yahuah empire, remain regionally contained, allow His covenant line through Shem to flourish, protect the birth of Abraham, preserve the promise of Mashiyach, and enable redemption history to proceed. The Tower of Babel is therefore not simply a morality tale, a judgment story, or an ancient myth; it is a critical salvation event that preserved the line of Yahusha.

9.8 – THE SECOND HUMANITY AFTER THE FLOOD

The second humanity survived through a hybrid vessel, descended from Mount Arrat, settled in Shinar (Senaar/Babel), built the first post-Flood hybrid empire, attempted to reenter the heavens, provoked Yahuah's merciful intervention, were scattered into the nations, formed the post-Flood giant lineages, and became the primary enemies of Yasharal. And through all of this, Yahuah protected His plan of redemption — from Noach to Shem to Eber to Abraham to Yahusha. Babel was darkness rising. Abraham

Chapter 10

The Three Equations Of Humanity

The Mathematical Revelation Of Purity, Corruption, And Redemption

10.1 – ONE HUMANITY BECOMES THREE

Humanity before the transgression of the Watchers existed as one unified group: the children of Adam and Chawwâh, bearing the Ruach of Yahuah, capable of covenant, obedience, righteousness, and redemption. But when the Watchers descended (Bereshith 6:1–4; 1 Enoch 6–7; Yôbêl 5:1–4), creation split into three spiritual categories, each defined by what they inherited — or did not inherit — from their fathers. These three equations govern the entire Bible:

why salvation is needed

why salvation is possible

why salvation is limited to Adam's line,

why Yahusha must come through a pure human genealogy.

They are not symbolic; they are spiritual biology — literal equations of Ruach and flesh.

10.2 – EQUATION 1: ANGELS WATCHERS + WOMEN = NEPHILIM

Watchers (no Ruach) plus human women (with Ruach) equals beings with no Ruach. This equation describes the creation of the Second Humanity — the Nephilim.

10.3 – SCRIPTURAL FOUNDATION

Bereshith 6:4 declares, "The Nephilim were in the earth in those days... mighty ones... men of renown." In 1 Enoch 15:3–7, Yahuah says, "You were spiritual... but you have defiled yourselves with the blood of women... you have produced children of flesh... they are born of the earth and have no Ruach." Yôbêl (Jubilees) 5:1 states, "The sons of Elohim... took women... and produced giants."

10.4 – WHY DO NEPHILIM HAVE NO RUACH?

Angels are spirits, not Adamic beings; they were never given the "nishmat chayyim" — the divine breath of life (Bereshith 2:7). They cannot transmit what they never received. Only Adam's line carries transmissible Ruach; the breath of Elohiym was given to Adam and flows through his line. Angels cannot father Ruach-bearing children. Thus hybrid beings inherit physical life but not spiritual life; they are physically alive, spiritually dead, and disconnected from covenant.

10.5 – HEAVEN'S TESTIMONY ABOUT THEM

1 Enoch and Jubilees describe them as "bastards," "spirits of wickedness," "corruptions of flesh," and "destroyers of the earth." Scripture calls them "Giants... mighty ones... men of renown" (Bereshith 6:4). Heaven calls them abominations, intrusions, corruptions of creation.

10.6 – RESULT OF EQUATION 1

Equation 1 creates the Second Humanity — beings with no Ruach, no covenant, no repentance, and no redemption. They stand completely outside the plan of salvation.

10.7 – EQUATION 2: NEPHILIM MEN + PURE WOMEN = NEPHILIM

A Nephilim father cannot transmit what he does not have. This equation explains why hybrid lines continued after the Flood.

1. — The Spiritual Law of Paternity

In Scripture, the father determines spiritual identity. Genesis genealogies say, "X begat Y" — lineage follows the father. The covenant is called "the Elohiym of Abraham, Yitschaq, and Ya'aqov"— fathers define covenant line. Thus, if the father has the Ruach, the child has access to the Ruach; if the father has no Ruach, the child cannot receive it. Yôbêl 7:21–24 confirms that the giants continued after the Flood through surviving hybrid lines.

2. — The Equation in Action

A Nephilim father with no Ruach and a pure Adamic mother with Ruach produce a child with no Ruach. The result is the same as Equation 1: no covenant capacity, no spiritual connection, no redemption.

3. — What This Explains

This equation explains why Repha'im, Emim, Anakim, and Zamzummim exist after the Flood, why Yahuah commanded their destruction (Debariym 2–3; Yahusha 11–12), why they could not be assimilated or redeemed, and why Yasharel's wars were often against giants.

4. — The Principle Remains

Nephilim reproduce Nephilim — "after their kind" (Bereshith 1). Corruption begets corruption. Death begets death.

10.8 – EQUATION 3: PURE MEN + NEPHILIM WOMEN = MIXED HUMANITY

A pure father transmits the Ruach; a Nephilim mother transmits corrupted flesh. This is the most complex equation. It explains almost all human civilization after Genesis 10.

1. — The Father's Side: Transmission of Ruach

When the father is from the line of Shem, Eber, Abraham, or other true Adamic carriers of the Ruach, the child receives divine breath, spiritual capacity, potential for covenant, and the ability to seek Elohiym.

2. — The Mother's Side: Transmission of Corruption

When the mother descends from Nephilim lines and carries hybrid DNA and spiritual corruption, the child inherits inclinations toward rebellion, dual nature, inner warfare, and tendencies toward occultism and idolatry.

3. — The Result: A Mixed Third Humanity

This child is half Adamic and half hybrid, spiritually alive because of the Ruach from the father but genetically and morally conflicted because of corruption from the mother. They become founders of idolatrous systems, builders of Babel and later empires, inventors of pagan religions, and architects of kingdoms that war against Yasharal. This third group fills the pages of Scripture as the nations.

10.9 – THE THEOLOGICAL WEIGHT OF THE THREE EQUATIONS

Together, the three equations explain why redemption is necessary, why redemption is limited to Adam's line, why Yasharal was chosen, why Yahusha must come through a pure genealogy, and why the end-times mirror the days of Noach.

1. — Why Redemption Is Necessary

Corruption (Equation 1 and 2) invaded creation and began spreading through lines never meant to exist.

2. — Why Redemption Is Limited to Adam's Line

Only the line with Ruach — the pure Adamic line — can respond to conviction, repentance, covenant, and Messiah. Nephilim have no Ruach and no redemption. Mixed humanity has Ruach but is conflicted; they can be redeemed but are easily corrupted.

3. — Why Yasharal Was Chosen

Yasharal was chosen to guard the pure line, the covenant, the prophecy, and the genealogy that leads to Yahusha.

4. — Why Yahusha Must Come Through a Pure Genealogy

Matthew 1 and Luke 3 trace a line from Adam to Sheth to Noach to Shem to Abraham to Dawid to Yahusha. Messiah must be fully Adamic, fully human, fully Ruach-bearing, and untouched by hybrid corruption.

5. — Why the End-Times Mirror the Days of Noach

Yahusha said, "As it was in the days of Noach, so shall it be also in the days of the Son of Man." — Luke 17:26. Daniel 2:43 prophesies, "They shall mingle themselves with the seed of men..." Hybrid corruption returns. The equations reappear. The conflict intensifies.

10.10 – THE THREE EQUATIONS RECAP

Equation 1: Angels watchers + Women = Nephilim

Angels watchers plus women equals Nephilim — no Ruach, no redemption, no covenant, second humanity, spiritually dead giants.

Equation 2: Nephilim Men + Pure Women = Nephilim

Nephilim men plus pure women equals Nephilim — corruption continues, father determines spiritual identity, offspring remain without Ruach, post-Flood giants explained.

Equation 3: Pure Men + Nephilim Women = Mixed Humanity

Pure men plus Nephilim women equals mixed humanity — Ruach transmitted through the father, corruption transmitted through the mother, child becomes spiritually conflicted, third humanity created, root of paganism, empire, and world religions.

10.11 – FINAL DECLARATION

These three equations are not mythology; they are the spiritual mathematics of history. They reveal how creation was divided, why the Bible follows only one line, why the nations are the way they are, why Yasharal is central, why Yahusha's genealogy matters, and why the final restoration will require the total removal of hybrid corruption. From here, we can move from explaining corruption to tracing redemption, as we follow the pure line — from Shem to Eber to Abraham — toward the ultimate fulfillment in Yahusha ha'Mashyach. The stage is ready for the Volume 2.

THE 22 WORKS OF CREATION CHART

Day	Work #	Work of Creation
Day 1	1	The Heavens
	2	The Waters
	3	Angels
	4	Spirit of Man
	5	Abyss

Day	Work #	Work of Creation
	6	Darkness
	7	Light
Day 2	8	Firmament
Day 3	9	Bodies of Water
	10	Mist / Dew
	11	Plants
	12	Garden of Eden
Day 4	13	Sun
	14	Moon
	15	Stars
Day 5	16	Leviathan
	17	Marine Life
	18	Birds
Day 6	19	Land Animals
	20	Livestock
	21	That Which Moves on the Earth
	22	Man

THE DIVISION OF SHEOL / SEOL CHART

Division	Description	Key Bible Verses
1. Garden of Eden (Paradise)	Resting place of the righteous; presence of life and peace	Luke 23:43; 2 Cor 12:2–4; Rev 2:7; Gen 2:8
2. Chambers of the Just (Abraham's Bosom)	Comfort for the righteous awaiting resurrection	Luke 16:22–25; Ps 116:15; Wis. 3:1
3. Chambers of the Martyrs	Souls of those slain for the testimony of Yahuah	Rev 6:9–11; Rev 20:4; Matt 5:10–12
4. Chambers of the Wicked	Sleep of the wicked before final judgment	Luke 16:23–24; Ps 9:17; Job 24:19; Isa 14:9–11
5. The Prison (Watchers & Demons)	Abyss where fallen angels and demons are bound	2 Pet 2:4; Jude 1:6; 1 Enoch 10:11–14; Rev 20:1–3
6. Lake of Fire (Lower Hell / Second Death)	Final eternal judgment; the second death	Rev 20:14–15; Matt 25:41; Rev 21:8; Mark 9:43–48

THE THREE HUMANITIES GRAPHICS

SHABBATH COMMANDS
FROM THE BOOK OF JUBILEES
THE SACRED SHABBATH

"A festival day and a qdosh day... a day of the qadosh kingdom forever."
(Jubilees 50:7-13)

PERMITTED ON THE SHABBATH

Personal Observance
- Eat what was prepared on the 6th day
- Drink what was prepared on the 6th day
- Rest from all labor
- Bless Yahugh
- Celebrate the Shabbath as a festival
- Treat the day as a *qadosh* (holy) day
- Be satisfied; enjoy the feast of the Shabbath

Temple-Only Priestly Work
(The only work permitted on Shabbat)
- Burning lebonah (incense)
- Bringing oblations
- Bringing sacrifices
- Offering atonement sacifices for Yashar'el

FINAL COMMAND
(Jubilees 50:13)

"Whoever does any of these things on Shabbath shall die.... that Yashar'el may observe the Shabbath

NOT PERMITTED ON THE SHABATH

General Actions
- Any manner of work
- Doing work not prepared on the 6th day
- Lying with one's woman (sexual relations)
- Declaring future work (?will do...

Buying, Selling, and Commerce
- Any buying or selling

Movement and Travel
- Setting out on an journey
- Traveling for any purpose
- Riding any beast
- Traveling by ship

Handling Burdens or Water
- Drawing water not prepared the day before
- Carrying any *burden* out of house or tent
- Making wat on Shabbat

Religious Misuse
- Killing any creature
- Siaughtering a beasst or bird
- Catching an anmal, bird or fish

GIANT TERRITORIES

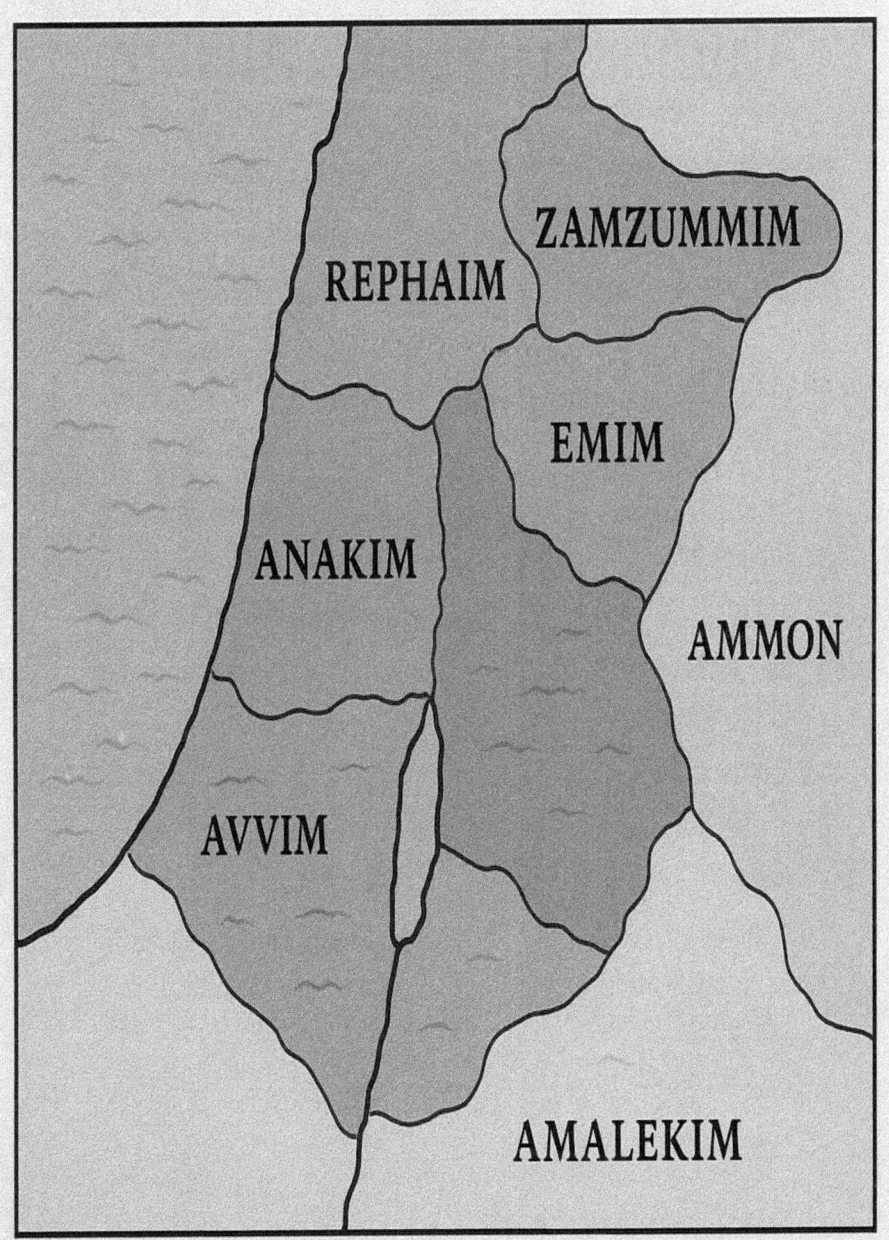

Anunnaki (Pagan) vs. Anakim

ANUNNAKI (PAGAN)	ANAKIM (SCRIPTURE)
• Claimed to be the "gods" of the ancient world.	• Were giants born through the union of fallen angels and women.
• Portrayed as creators who "descended from the heavens."	• Transgressed by corrupting the creation of Yahuah.
• Revered as brilliant, wise, and advanced "teachers" of mankind.	• Existed as foreign hybrid enemies of the covenant people.
• Gained fame through archaeological theories and ancient astronaut ideas.	• Called "**sons of the giant**" and "children of the Nephilim."
• Promoted as benevolent beings who evolved humanity.	• Identified as enemies who opposed the redemptive plan.

THE THREE HUMANITIES – FULL MUSIC ALBUM

🎵 SONG 1 🎵

THE 22 WORKS OF CREATION

🎵 Verse 1 —

Hear now the mystery sealed in the first seven days,

for the beginning is the prophecy of the end,

and creation is the scroll on which salvation was first written.

🎵 Chorus — The Light Revealed

DAY ONE — THE LIGHT OF THE LAMB

Before sun or star,

before moon or flame,

the Light shone forth —

Yahusha, the Eternal Radiance,

the Lamb slain from the foundation.

In His Light, creation awakens;

in His brightness, all things begin.

🎵 Verse 2 — Holy Distinction

DAY TWO — THE GREAT SEPARATION

The Firmament spread out like a canopy,

dividing the waters above from the waters below.

Thus Yahuah revealed the decree of holiness:

the clean from the unclean,

the righteous from the wicked,

the heaven-born from the earth-bound.

Salvation begins with distinction.

🎵 Chorus — The Garden Prepared

DAY THREE —

Dry land rose from the deep

as resurrection from the grave,

and Eden was planted before the dust of Adam was formed.

A garden made ready in advance —

a shadow of the world restored

for the redeemed of Elyôn.

🎵 Verse 3 — Signs in the Heavens

DAY FOUR — THE SIGNS OF REDEMPTION

The great lights were appointed:

the sun to rule the day,

the moon and stars to rule the night.

Not for beauty alone,

but for Mo'edim — the appointed times,

the prophetic calendar of the Messiah.

In the heavens, the story of redemption is marked and measured.

🎵 Chorus — Life Overflowing

DAY FIVE — THE MULTIPLICATION OF LIFE

The seas swarmed, the skies filled,

and blessing overflowed upon the

creatures.

Life multiplied at the command of Yahuah,

a whisper of the age to come

when abundance and peace shall fill the earth.

🎵 *Verse 4 — The Image Bearer*

DAY SIX —

From the dust came Adam,

shaped by Elohiym's hands,

filled with the breath of life.

Created to rule, created pure,

yet chosen for restoration through the Second Adam — Yahusha,

the Perfect Image and the Perfect King.

🎵 *Bridge — Eternal Rest*

DAY SEVEN — THE ETERNAL SABBATH

And Yahuah rested.

The crown of creation,

the sign of the Kingdom,

the promise of the world to come.

A Shabbath without end,

a day that shall swallow all days,

the reign of Yahusha in everlasting peace.

🎵 *Final Chorus — The Pattern Revealed*

Behold the pattern:

Creation.

Separation.

Preparation.

Revelation.

Multiplication.

Restoration.

Kingdom.

In the 22 Works of Creation,

the whole plan is revealed.

The first week is the prophecy of the last.

Genesis is the Gospel in its oldest form.

The Lamb stands at the beginning,

and reigns at the end.

Thus ends the Sacred Scroll of the First Week.

Blessed is he who reads,

and blessed is he who understands.

◇◇◇◇◇◇◇◇◇◇◇◇◇◇◇◇◇◇◇◇

🎵 SONG 2 🎵

WHEN HUMANITY BREAK

INTRO —

WHEN HUMANITY BREAK

Book Three will not retell the purity of the First Humanity.

It will reveal how the Second Humanity emerges,

how the inner tensions and external temptations finally collide,

how the Watchers' rebellion tears into the human story,

how the nature of mankind is challenged, altered, and weaponized,

and how Yahuah's redemption plan responds to this new, brutal reality.

VERSE 1 — What Book Three Will Uncover

If Book One revealed the Works of Creation,

and Book Two revealed the First Humanity in its holy beginning,

then Book Three will uncover:

The Fallen Nature —

How the Second Humanity Was Born,

and How Yahuah Refused to Abandon His Design.

VERSE 2 — The Shift in the Story

The story now moves from untested purity to assaulted identity,

from uncontested order to spiritual war,

from quiet preparation to open conflict.

The First Humanity has been prepared.

The stage is set.

Heaven has watched.

The testimony is written.

PRE-CHORUS — The Question Rises

Now the question will be tested

in the world of the Second Humanity:

What happens when a pure creation

meets a corruption it was never designed to host?

CHORUS — Standing on the Edge

What happens when a pure creation

meets a corruption it was never designed to host?

What happens when the First Humanity

stands on the threshold of darkness?

Book Two ends here —

with the First Humanity standing in the light of Yahuah,

on the very edge of a darkness

that will try — and fail — to erase everything Yahuah has begun.

FINAL CHORUS — Darkness Will Fail

Book Two ends here —

with the First Humanity standing in the light of Yahuah,

on the very edge of a darkness

that will try — and fail — to erase everything Yahuah has begun.

What happens when a pure creation

meets a corruption it was never designed to host?

WHEN HUMANITY BREAKS —

Yahuah refuses to abandon His design.

OUTRO — The Coming War

The story now moves

from untested purity to assaulted identity,

from uncontested order to spiritual war,

from quiet preparation to open conflict.

The First Humanity has been prepared.

The stage is set.

◇◇◇◇◇◇◇◇◇◇◇◇◇◇◇◇◇◇

🎵 SONG 3 🎵

THE SPIRITUAL MATHEMATICS OF HISTORY

INTRO —

These three equations are not mythology; they are the spiritual mathematics of history.

VERSE 1 — What They Reveal

They reveal how creation was divided,

why the Bible follows only one line,

why the nations are the way they are,

why Yasharal is central,

why Yahusha's genealogy matters,

and why the final restoration will require the total removal of hybrid corruption.

CHORUS — From Explanation to Revelation

From here, we can move from explaining corruption

to tracing redemption,

as we follow the pure line —

from Shem to Eber to Abraham —

toward the ultimate fulfillment in Yahusha ha'Mashyach.

BRIDGE —

These three equations are not mythology;

they are the spiritual mathematics of history.

They reveal how creation was divided.

They reveal why Yasharal is central.

They reveal why Yahusha's genealogy matters.

They reveal why the final restoration

will require the total removal of hybrid corruption.

FINAL CHORUS — Redemption Unfolds

From here, we can move from explaining corruption

to tracing redemption,

as we follow the pure line —

from Shem to Eber to Abraham —

toward the ultimate fulfillment in Yahusha ha'Mashyach.

OUTRO — The Story Moves Forward

Toward the ultimate fulfillment

in Yahusha ha'Mashyach.

🎵 SONG 4 🎵

THE MERCY OF YAHUAH IN A DIVIDED HUMANITY

VERSE 1 — A World Divided

THE MERCY OF YAHUAH IN A DIVIDED HUMANITY

How Redemption Survived the Rise of the Second Humanity

Part two of this volume unveils one of the most dramatic and dangerous eras in all of creation:

the moment humanity split into two opposing lines — one created by Yahuah, and one created through forbidden unions between angels and women.

It is the darkest rupture in human history.

It is the moment when:

• purity met corruption,

• light met darkness,

• covenant met rebellion,

• the first humanity met the second humanity.

CHORUS — The Triumph of Mercy

Yet even in this crisis of world proportions, the truth that emerges is not the triumph of evil —

but the triumph of mercy.

Let every reader understand this unmovable reality:

Yahuah's mercy is stronger than human failure,

stronger than angelic rebellion,

stronger than the corruption of creation.

VERSE 2 —

Humanity Failed — But Yahuah Never Abandoned His Creation

From the beginning, humanity has stumbled:

• Adam fell — but Yahuah covered him with skins.

• Humanity drifted — but Yahuah raised Seth's righteous line.

• The world forgot righteousness — but Yahuah sent Enoch as king, priest, prophet, and teacher.

• The Watchers corrupted the earth — but Yahuah raised Noach.

• The nations united in rebellion at Babel — but Yahuah scattered them to preserve the covenant line.

VERSE 3 — What Yahuah Provided

At every moment of collapse, Yahuah provided:

• a covering

• a remnant

• a redeemer

• a righteous man

• a covenant

• a path forward

This is the theme of Part two:

Humanity fails repeatedly —

but Yahuah's mercy remains undefeated.

VERSE 4 — The Rise of the Second Humanity

The Rise of the Second Humanity Should Have Ended the Story — But It Didn't

The creation of the Nephilim — the second, hybrid humanity — was the greatest threat the world had ever faced.

They were:

• spiritually dead

• violently dominant

• genetically corrupted

- unable to repent
- incapable of covenant
- filled with the rebellion of their angelic fathers
- destroyers of all flesh

They consumed:

- humanity,
- animals,
- crops,
- each other,
- the earth itself.

It was extinction-level corruption.

BRIDGE — But Yahuah Was Not Defeated

Yet Yahuah was not defeated.

Instead He revealed a two-part redemptive plan:

CHORUS — The Triumph of Mercy

Yet even in this crisis of world proportions, the truth that emerges is not the triumph of evil —

but the triumph of mercy.

Let every reader understand this unmovable reality:

Yahuah's mercy is stronger than human failure,

stronger than angelic rebellion,

stronger than the corruption of creation.

♪ SONG 5 ♪

♪ THE TWO-PART MERCY OF YAHUAH —

VERSE 1 — The Last Righteous Branch

PART One - Preserve the Pure Seed Through Noach

Noach became the last righteous branch of Adam.

The ark was built not only to save life —

but to protect the genealogy through which Messiah would come.

Without Noach:

- no Abraham
- no Yitshaq
- no Yaaqob
- no Yasharal
- no Dawid
- no lineage of Yahudah
- no Yahusha

The entire plan of salvation was carried inside one man — and Yahuah preserved him.

CHORUS — The Seed Must Live

Noach became the last righteous branch of Adam,

the ark was built not only to save life —

but to protect the genealogy through which Messiah would come.

The entire plan of salvation was carried inside one man —

and Yahuah preserved him.

VERSE 2 — Waters of Mercy

Remove the Corrupted Seed Through the Flood

The flood was not divine anger.

It was divine mercy.

It was:

- a cleansing,

- a rescue,

- a surgical judgment,

- a protective shield around the future of redemption.

The flood saved the world from total hybridization.

It saved the possibility of salvation itself.

REFRAIN — Mercy in the Waters

The flood was not divine anger.

It was divine mercy.

A cleansing, a rescue, a surgical judgment,

a protective shield around the future of redemption.

VERSE 3 —

After the Flood — Mercy Still Reigned

The hybrid line survived through one vessel and migrated into Shinar.

There they:

- built Babel,

- reassembled forbidden knowledge,

- attempted to invade the heavens,

- created the first post-Flood empire of rebellion.

Once again, humanity approached annihilation.

Once again, Yahuah intervened.

This time, not with water — but with languages.

He confused their speech.

He shattered their unity.

He scattered them across the earth.

This was not a curse.

This was protection.

Babel's fall was the salvation of humanity.

BRIDGE —

Once again, humanity approached annihilation.

Once again, Yahuah intervened —

not with water, but with languages.

He confused their speech.

He shattered their unity.

He scattered them across the earth.

FINAL CHORUS — Salvation in the Shattering

This was not a curse.

This was protection.

Babel's fall was the salvation of humanity.

The flood saved the world from total hybridization.

It saved the possibility of salvation itself.

And the entire plan of salvation was carried inside one man —

and Yahuah preserved him.

🎵 SONG 6 🎵

🎵 THE TRIUMPH OF MERCY

INTRO

The Wisdom of Yahuah

The Three Equations Reveal the Wisdom of Yahuah

Through the three equations of humanity, we discover that:

- Yahuah never loses control,
- corruption cannot erase His purpose,
- rebellion cannot cancel His covenant,
- mixture cannot destroy His plan.

They show:

- where corruption came from,
- why it spread,
- how Yahuah preserved the pure seed,
- and how the story moves inevitably toward the Messiah.

These equations are the mathematical foundation of redemption.

VERSE 1 — Mercy Overcomes Every Darkness

Part Two Ends With the Triumph of Mercy — Not the Triumph of Evil

Despite:

- two humanities,
- the rise of giants,
- the spread of hybrid nations,
- angelic rebellion,
- global violence,
- the arrogance of Babel —

Yahuah's mercy prevailed.

The covenant survived.

The seed survived.

The promise survived.

The plan survived.

The darkness rose like a flood —

but Yahuah raised a higher standard.

REFRAIN — A Higher Standard

The covenant survived.

The seed survived.

The promise survived.

The plan survived.

The darkness rose like a flood —

but Yahuah raised a higher standard.

CHORUS — The Foundation of Redemption

Yahuah never loses control.

Corruption cannot erase His purpose.

Rebellion cannot cancel His covenant.

Mixture cannot destroy His plan.

These equations are the mathematical foundation of redemption.

VERSE 2 — The Destiny of Creation

THE DESTINY OF CREATION
BELONGS TO Yahuah

Part Two reveals the terrifying rise of the second humanity,

but even more importantly:

It reveals the unstoppable mercy of Yahuah.

He will always:

• protect His people

• preserve His covenant

• guard His promises

• raise a redeemer

• fulfill His Word

• carry the pure seed toward salvation

Nothing:

• not Watchers,

• not giants,

• not Babel,

• not rebellion,

• not corruption,

• not nations,

• not darkness —

can overthrow His purpose.

BRIDGE — Nothing Can Overthrow His Purpose

Nothing —

not Watchers, not giants, not Babel,

not rebellion, not corruption, not nations,

not darkness —

can overthrow His purpose.

FINAL VERSE — The Emergence of the Third Humanity

And now the world stands on the edge of a new reality:

The Third Humanity emerges —

a mixture of Ruach and corruption,

a battlefield of two natures,

and the stage upon which the next phase of redemption will unfold.

Volume 2 begins.

FINAL CHORUS —

He will always protect His people,

preserve His covenant,

guard His promises,

raise a redeemer,

fulfill His Word,

carry the pure seed toward salvation.

THE DESTINY OF CREATION
BELONGS TO Yahuah.

www.ingramcontent.com/pod-product-compliance
Lightning Source LLC
Chambersburg PA
CBHW070536090426
42735CB00013B/2998